Dodge #9:

HOW TO
NEVER MAKE A MISTAKE

*Achieving Success in a World That Is
Always Looking for Someone to Blame*

SHELDON B. SOSNA

Published by Hats Off Books
601 East 1st Street
Tucson, Arizona 85705 U.S.A.
www.hatsoffbooks.com

International Standard Book Number: 1-58736-020-9
Library of Congress Card Number: 00-111230

Cover and book design by Atilla Vékony
Illustrations by Jim Link

Printed in the United States of America

Table of Contents

Preface

This is a handbook designed to help readers achieve success in business. It is based on almost half a century of observation and participation in the formal choreography of making it to the pinnacle in the corporate world. As a management consultant, advertising executive and dedicated keyhole listener, I have been able to discover and synthesize the strategic machinations used by those who have managed to bubble to the top in their companies. Now you will be able to use these tactics, too.

Our studies have helped us determine that there are only two ways for anyone to achieve great success in the business world.

The first is to truly deserve that success. Those who do so just know more than the rest of us. They are the men and women who created the winning strategies, the blockbuster products, and the innovative financial ploys that defined the prosperity of their companies. They are the ones who get written up in *Fortune*, *The Wall Street Journal* and *Forbes*. But as you have probably observed, there are not many of these stars in real life.

The second, and much more frequent, path to success is to simply keep your head down, stay out of trouble and never get caught on the wrong side of a business decision. Eventually, if you persist in this behavior, you have a good chance of rising to the executive suite of your company. We have labeled this strategy "Dodge #9."

Those few who have already achieved that dream know that the secret of their success is embodied in the four magical words that are at the core of Dodge #9: "Never Make a Decision." Those who can master the art of remaining decisionless throughout their business careers can reach the nirvana promised on the cover of this book: Never Make a Mistake.

Introduction

The Dodges — Nine Ways to Avoid Paying the Piper

A dodge is an out, and excuse, a way to avoid paying the piper.

All of us are faced in life with situations we'd like to get out of, guilt we'd like to foist onto others, responsibilities we'd like to avoid. To allow us to do that, we have all perfected certain "dodges" that we use whenever we find ourselves in uncomfortable situations.

After a long and successful career in business, the author has discovered that there are just nine general categories of dodges. We list them in Appendix A. You can look at them now if you wish.

But it is Dodge #9 that is the most important for anyone seeking success in the world of business and commerce. For anyone who can master Dodge #9, the other eight dodges are unnecessary.

Here then — Dodge #9 — the Golden Path to success in the world of dollars and cents.

Part I

Avoiding Mistakes by Avoiding Decisions

Chapter One

Dodge #9 — The Golden Secret

Management 101

As every red-blooded MBA knows, you don't have to be an astrophysicist to outshine the men and women who today rule America's corporate hierarchy. Many young people, just starting their careers in business, are convinced that any idiot could do a better job of management than the person who now sits in the corner office at their company.

All of us, of course, have worked for bosses who didn't seem to have a clue. We've been appalled by their inability to make rational decisions. We've been shocked by their apparent confusion in the face of crisis. We've sometimes wondered how they manage to get dressed in the morning, let alone manage their awesome responsibilities. They must be dumb, we think. Or very lucky.

What we have never considered is the possibility that they are doing it all on purpose! It's not that most business leaders can't make rational decisions, *it's that they don't want to!*

How can that be?

This book will explain. And set you on the path to that penthouse office you'd like one day to occupy.

You see, most of the people who have made it to the top in your company, and in many others like it, have learned a very important secret that you must learn, too. It's called

Dodge #9. This open-sesame of business success is not some magical abracadabra beyond the ken of most men and women. On the contrary, the first element of Dodge #9 is so outrageously simple that it can be stated in its entirety in just four words:

Never Make a Mistake!

Yes, it's true. The fastest way to achieve success in any endeavor is to avoid making mistakes. The person who errs least goes farthest. The executive who never makes a mistake is the one who gets the office with the biggest window. Logical.

But how can anyone live a life without mistakes? It's not possible, you think. Yet, when you dig into it, you quickly realize that the only way to avoid making any errors is to avoid making any decisions. If you are without decision, you are without sin. Which brings us to the second element of Dodge #9:

Never Make a Decision!

So the boss you have always thought of as spineless because he can't seem to make up his mind is really being very wise. He is not making decisions because he knows that by delegating decision-making to others, he can never get caught on the wrong side of any business situation. That spells success.

How, you ask, can a business executive hold his job without ever saying yes or no to any question, without pointing in one direction or another and shouting "Onward" to his troops?

He can do it because he knows that indecision — Dodge #9 — is the smartest decision of all.

And he does it very cleverly, by letting you, his subordinate, make his decisions for him. The result: the Boss gets the credit if your decision — against all odds — happens to be right. (After all, he or she was smart enough to hire you in the first place.) And only you get the blame when your decision turns out to be a disaster. ("Well," the boss tells you during the separation interview, "you were given the chance to excel, but just couldn't cut it. Too bad.")

Now the really diabolical part of this make-it-to-the-top strategy is that young people coming into the company are actually encouraged to boldly make the decisions that their managers are loathe to risk. So it's no wonder that every business school grad who decides to trade faded campus Levi's for a three-piece business suit, and follow dear old dad up the corporate ladder, expects to make it to the top in the world of commerce in a hurry. After all, his boss seems to think that anything he says is brilliant!

And who can argue with the new kid, given his unquestioned aptitude with Microsoft Word, Excel, Quicken, Java and the Internet? To say nothing of all he or she learned in college about the arts of intimidation, negotiation, and the wearing of nifty casual clothes?

But the sad fact (as new recruits soon learn) is that none of these important skills—or any of the hundreds of others that he or she mastered at University Business School—is going to be more than mildly helpful in achieving their objective: a top spot in the world of business. For while he or she may have developed a great deal of talent in finance, administration, production and marketing, and can speak the argot of the business world like a natural-born native, the chances are that these young men and women are completely ignorant when it comes to the most important talent of all, the talent without which everything else must come to naught: Dodge #9—Indecision.

This one basic rule of business is far more important than mere college knowledge to the person who wants to get to the top. It is more important than brains, talent, personality, good looks or family connection. It is even more important than independent wealth. It is, in truth, *the* most important factor in helping a man or woman achieve success in the business world.

And yet, only a tiny handful of the people who each year enter into this world are even aware that Dodge #9 exists at all—no matter how many advanced college degrees they have managed to accumulate.

Most young men and women eagerly beginning a business career spend the first few years cautiously feeling their way and getting the superficial gloss that a successful business life requires: eating with the right fork, ordering the proper gin in a martini, making the most of petty cash, carrying a cell phone clapped to an ear while hurrying no place.

"What did you do at the office today?" their young spouses eagerly ask each evening. "Oh," the executive trainee casually responds, "I had vichyssoise with a vice president for lunch." Obviously a person on the way up.

But, after a few years of snail-paced advancement, the wiser and more perceptive of these young people begin to sense some lack; begin to have the uneasy feeling that, perhaps, being able to do a ginger-peachy job of preparing a profit and loss analysis, a nifty business plan, or an acrobatic production schedule, is not the be-all and end-all of making it to the pinnacle in his or her company. These talents alone, it slowly begins to dawn on them, are not going to bring them the success of which they so fondly dreamt. There must be something else, they begin to realize, that sends some people careening up the express elevator of success, while others seem to mark time forever trying to inch up the down escalator of failure.

A few lucky ones eventually stumble onto the Dodge #9 secret. They find it either through an innate sensitivity of their own, or because some wise and kindly mentor takes pity and drops a fatherly word.

But, sadly, most men and women entering the world of commerce and industry never find the answer, never dis-

I had vichyssoise with a vice president for lunch

cover this vital bit of knowledge. Their career curves flatten and dangle. Like Dilbert, they remain forever imprisoned in windowless inside cubicles and accumulate an embarrassing number of years in grade. Eventually, they're given their retirement Bulova and retreat to Florida for their golden years. A wiser few manage to prolong the process, jolting their career curves upward for brief additional spans of time by making a judicious job change or two. But the Bulova always catches up with them at last, somewhere in the teaming middle levels of business life. Their vichyssoise turns to potato soup.

That's a shame. This handbook was written to help you achieve success in business. It will show you how others have managed to use Dodge #9 to get where they wanted to go.

Go thou and do likewise.

Giving the Office Boy Decision-Making Status

Brand Manager is a title that many new fresh new MBAs strive to achieve when they get their first shot at the business big time. What few of them realize is that the title they are so anxious to have is not a badge of corporate honor but just a synonym for expendable.

The reason is that many big companies seek continuing growth through continuing product proliferation. They bring out twenty or more new items a year and hope that at least one manages to find a niche in the market.

Each such product effort requires its own brand manager, and companies traditionally assign the title to bright new hires, fresh from Harvard or Princeton or Northwestern. The thinking is that a new graduate probably is up-to-date on all the latest thinking in marketing and management, and has the diploma to prove it, so the product won't suffer from any lack of basic business knowledge on the part of its brand manager. It will therefore either break or make it to the market based on its own merits. And no one in higher management will need to make a decision that could later cripple his or her career. The young brand manager is, by definition, responsible for all decisions relating to that product.

One major multi-branded cigarette manufacturer (in the days before cigarettes were labeled with a skull and crossbones) used to hand out brand manager titles to its greenest recruits as if they were lollipops. The company would recruit the brightest and best business school graduates every year by promising each a brand manager title as soon as they showed up at the front door, shiny new cordovan leather briefcase in hand.

These kids were always handsome, clean-cut and eager to make their mark. Their chests would heave with pride when, four days after seeing their names engraved on a black plastic desk plaque, the division chief dropped into their spanking new offices and said something like, "John (or Bill or Steve; there were few young women in those days), we have this new cigarette brand we're very excited about. We're planning to bring it to market very soon and I think you are just the man to manage it through to the market. Congratulations."

Can you imagine the excitement when this new recruit bragged to his young wife about his good fortune that evening? Wasn't corporate life exciting!

But what these young MBAs don't realize is, first, that their chances for success are minuscule and, second, that their titles should have been Fatted Calf instead of brand manager. It is all a setup. These new executives may know all there is to know about the latest in marketing and manufacturing technology, but they are no match for the sales executives, the ad agency honchos, the media reps, the package design creatives and others with whom they must joust daily and who try to manipulate them. They haven't learned what their real objectives should be—to avoid making any decisions about their new product at all. Success or failure of the new product is out of their hands no matter what they do. The Laws of Chance are in charge.

By simply sitting back and letting the ad agency, the sales department, the label designers and the promotion specialists go wherever the hell they want to go, the young brand manager has a fifty-fifty chance that his new brand will be a success. Of course, he must do this by appearing to be deliberative about each decision, but in the end, just letting it go to the loudest bidder.

If the new brand somehow achieves a .05 share of market, he will be slapped on the back and the now successful brand will be assigned to one of the "real" brand managers, men who have been lurking around the corner and waiting. If it isn't a success, the young sacrificial brand manager will be offered a chance to resign gracefully or become someone's assistant. No more black plastic name plate.

If he's clever, he will be able to parlay his brand manager title at Company A into a brand manager title at Company B, where, it is hoped, he will put into practice what he so painfully learned in his first job.

DODGE #9:

To Never Make a Mistake

NEVER MAKE A DECISION!

* Although they are only nine words,
they are important enough to deserve
a page of their own. You might want to
cut this page out of the book and have it
framed for your office wall.

Chapter Two

Just How Hard Is It?

Avoiding Decisions Forever

"Never make a decision!"

It sounds too simple, you say? You don't believe it? You refuse to accept the idea that these few words are actually the fabled Dodge #9, the Golden Secret of Business Success that people whisper about. All right. We respect your skepticism. So we offer you this simple two-step proof:

1. As everyone knows, advancement in business can best be measured not by salary level but by the amount of *decision-making authority* that a business person can gather into his or her own hands.[*] In other words, the *right to make decisions* is the most important gauge of a person's importance in the business scheme of things. The more decisions a man or woman is in a position to

---

[*] Lots of people think that salary is the key measure of power. It really isn't. While a high salary and top authority often go together, this isn't always so. Too many variables affect salary: seniority, nepotism, competition for talent. Sometimes you pay a guy a lot of loot just to keep him in a lowly position, doing a job no one else wants to do. People who think they are negotiating their way upward in a company by asking for more money rather than more authority are not very smart. They deserve the grudging raises they get, and the early career stagnation that soon sets in!

make, the more senior that person is in the organization!

Indeed, the topmost job in any organization is the one
where all the decision authority comes to rest, in the
hands of one supreme executive. It's where the buck
stops. That's why it is more important to be the Chief
Executive Officer in a company than to be its Chairman
of the Board!

Thus, advancement in business can be defined as the
accumulation of decision-authority. Agreed? So far, so
good.

2. But how does one go about gathering decision-
authority unto one's self?

Experience shows, as we've said, that the one sure way
for the average man or woman in business to accumulate power and authority is to avoid making mistakes;
to never get caught on the down side of a business "situation." In short, to never be wrong is the genius of
Dodge #9. While brain surgeons, senators and DNA
researchers are given the right to make a mistake or two
in life, there is no such forgiveness in business. The less
often you are wrong, the more authority you are given
and the higher you climb.

And if you are *never wrong*, you go all the way.

However, a moment's reflection will tell you that the
only way to never be wrong is to never have an opinion
that can possibly have a consequence.

"Isn't there a contradiction here?" you ask. "In one
paragraph you advise us to gather as much decision-
authority as possible, and, in the next paragraph, advise
against actually making decisions!"

But the two paragraphs are not contradictory at all!
There is a vast, though subtle, difference between responsi-

Responsibility is the nakedness of the sure loser

bility and authority. Authority—the *right* to do something—is the garb of the business winner. Responsibility—
actually *doing* something—is the nakedness of the sure
loser. To be successful, a person must understand the difference.

That is what Dodge #9 is all about.

But simply understanding the difference is not enough.
You must learn to use the difference to your own advantage. That can be tricky. It takes only a few words to state
the basic principle behind Dodge #9: In order to never
make a mistake, you must never make a decision.

But it will take this whole volume to teach the techniques involved in applying this principle to your own
business career.

Of course, some readers will complain that the facts of
business life are not what we state them to be. There will be
those who hold that this little book preaches a cynical and
negative doctrine. In support of their position, they will cite
the hallowed names of men who, through the adroit use of
their decision-making skills, have advanced to the pinnacle
of success in both public and business life. The names of
folk heroes like Bill Gates, Warren Buffet, Michael Eisner
and Ross Perot will be invoked in denial of the thesis of this
text.

Our reply is simple:

"All right," we say. "Go ahead and *be* Tom Watson or
Samuel Goldwyn or Peter Lynch or Liddy Dole—if you
can. But before you try it, please notice how few Henry
Fords the world has produced, and how many people like
you!"

Chapter Three

The Dangers of Decision & the Perils of the Twenty-First Century

"YOU are responsible for this!"

Read those dire words again. And yet again. They make up the second most dreaded phrase in business life today![*] If you can avoid having them addressed to you, you have an unlimited future ahead of you. If you can't, you don't.

No decisions, no responsibility. It's the only way you can be sure that you will never make a mistake.

But while it may sound easy to do, applying Dodge #9 to your business career is really very difficult! Most authorities concede that it is much harder to make *no decisions* than it is to make *right decisions*. It takes the concentration of a chess grandmaster, the caution of a fugitive and the street smarts of a Three-Card Monte artist to avoid the decision-making traps that business life sets for us every day.

Paradoxically, to be successfully indecisive requires that you be very decisive! You can't be wishy-washy about being wishy-washy. You must learn to stand firm about not standing firm.

---

* The first most dreaded phrase is, of course, "You're fired!" It usually comes right after the phrase being discussed. As a matter of fact, some authorities say that both sentences together really constitute a single phrase since they are almost always twinned.

17

In fact, learning to make no decision at all is so immensely difficult, even for the dedicated expert, that few men or women in business life can achieve perfection at it without many years of practice in the application of the principles set forth in this text. That's why CEOs are usually old guys.

It's going to get worse. This new century will exponentially expand the number of pitfalls waiting to swallow you up. For example, think of the problems associated with learning to make money on the Internet, certain to be one of the most important corporate objectives in the 2000s. If you are not very cautious, you could blow a couple of hundred mil just getting your company up on its own web site. Many big companies on the Internet already have.

Beware, too, of all the new developments in computing technology that will be speeding toward you in the new century. They could bite you when you're not looking. For example, being put in charge of buying computers for any company will be less than a thankless job, because it will invariably come with a pink slip. Since change and obsolescence occur so fast these days, six months after management's initial enthusiasm for the new machines you purchased, the refrain will become, "Why couldn't he have waited six months to get the very latest."[*] You won't even know why you've been downsized!

That's only the beginning. What about selecting the best communication system for your company? Will you go wired, wireless, fiber-optic, cable, or satellite? Will you buy phones or beepers or go cellular? Or opt for communications technologies not yet imagined?

Marketing and advertising protocols will be changing too. What if you spend your whole ad budget in an ad

---

[*] A new generation of computer technology erupts every three months on average. While you are busy buying expensive 900-megahertz machines, Intel is already tooling up for the new Pentium VI 2,000-meg processor due out next month.

medium that nobody looks at anymore? Do you go with print, TV, or on the Internet? Do you go direct mail or e-mail? What if the mass mailing you develop comes back all zeroes? Nobody really knows which media New Consumers will use to gather the information that will guide their purchase patterns in the 2000s. Surely not you.

New kinds of open employment options are now being tested for the new century, including work-at-home, shared jobs, consulting, executive outsourcing, etc. But what if your superior asks you to move your company to a low-rent district in order to save money for stockholders? You will earn congratulations at first, until everyone discovers that there are no good restaurants in a warehouse district. Not a Starbucks in sight. Tough. Go directly to jail.

And it goes on. New generations of automobiles are coming. New kinds of building materials are being developed. New financial instruments and strategies are being invented. Round-the-clock day trading. New kinds of electronic gadgetry are turning up at Circuit City and Best Buy every few days. Wireless is what's happening. New entertainment options keep popping up as quickly as Disney and DreamWorks and Lucasfilm can invent them up. New kinds of movies, new generations of sitcoms, new kinds of music delivery systems, new kinds of theme parks, new ways to entertain clients, new ways to screw around after dark—it never ends. New attitudes about morality are changing the way we look at life. New ways to invest are compounding the many ways we already have to lose our inheritance. The opportunities to fail keep expanding

Guess wrong in any of these arenas, and you quickly slide to the bottom of the heap.

In addition to all of these new opportunities to screw up in the 2000s, the new technologies available will make it harder than ever to keep your mistakes hidden from management. In the past, you may have been able to avoid decision-responsibility by simply telling a few strategic lies from time to time. Now, no matter what you say, your hard disk will know the truth. And your e-mail will catch you up. No place to hide. Sorry.

So the problems of remaining decisionless in the future are greater than anyone expected them to be. It's going to be tough. Maybe you won't be able to do it. We'll try to help.*

It is understandable that, with all of the traps attendant on learning how not to make decisions, the shortsighted (or lazy!) may come to feel that it would somehow be easier to learn to make *right decisions* instead of *no decisions at all.*

Yes, it would be easier. But it would definitely not be better, for several very good reasons. The first is that the timeworn bromide that preaches, "You only have to be right 51% of the time to achieve success," is nothing more than an old wives' tale. Experience shows that correct decisions are *never* remembered for more than three working days and never over a weekend, so they count for nothing. But wrong decisions are remembered forever, no matter how unimportant they may have seemed at the time. Make one bad call in a thousand during your career, and you are sure to be remembered as a wrongo till the end of time. Those odds are much too steep, even for you. You've heard the story often, in one context or another:

> He: "There goes old Thompson — poor guy."

> She: "I always thought he was one of the most promising men in the whole company. What happened?"

---

* Because of the difficulty of maintaining an utterly decisionless stance, this book contains a final section especially written for those who, in spite of their most vigilant efforts, backslide into an occasional unequivocality. This final section will provide you with a compendium of tested methods for escaping responsibility even for those things for which you are, in fact, responsible.

A wrong decision is remembered forever!

He: "Poor devil ordered Mac software for the
    IBM computers!"

She: "Well, you really never know what a man
    is made of until the chips are down!"

Another reason it is better to make no decisions instead
of right decisions is that most people can't tell a right decision from a wrong one. So even if the decision you make is
right, you will still have just as many people against you as
for you. If you make no decision, nobody will be against
you.

Third, even the most correct decisions have a way of
turning into incorrect decisions after the fact. Ask any politician. There is no final judgment one can hide behind.
You've seen it happen a hundred times: yesterday's war
hero is today's war monger; yesterday's fashion fad is
today's grunge; yesterday's perfect gentleman is today's
sexist pig. And did you see your old college sweetheart at
the last class reunion? Ugh! History has a way of ridiculing
her champions eventually.

Finally, you must never forget that the success of any
decision does not depend on whether it is the right decision, but on *how it affects the careers and aspirations of those
around you.*

Consider the many conflicting elements that must come
together harmoniously in order to make a decision successful:

• A good decision must solve a problem that may not be
recognized as a problem by everyone concerned; or, if it is
recognized as a problem, the problem may be defined
differently by different people. Or not defined at all!

Boss: "Say, Jones, why did you suddenly decide
    to make all the wheels on these automobiles
    round? Is that what you meant to do? I don't
    understand...."

• A good decision must mesh with various facts, opinions and requirements—not all of which may be available to you when you are making the decision.

> Boss: "Ms. Smith, I thought you knew that the
>   Board of Directors has decided that we
>   didn't need to spend any funds on develop-
>   ing a new product line."

• A good decision must please the people who judge the decision, even though the basis for their judgment is seldom known to the decision-maker.

> You: "Do you think this is what old Smith is
>   looking for?"

> Associate: "Who the hell knows!"

• And a good decision must also please the people who will be in charge of implementing it, and who will be pleased not by what the decision does for the problem that occasioned it, but by what it does—and doesn't do—for them.

> Boss: "Simpkins, don't you know that by build-
>   ing that science lab right there, you have
>   made it impossible for me to have my new
>   executive elevator installed? I really hate
>   that."

> You: "Sorry, sir. I had it all wrong."

• A good decision must also please the people who will be affected by the final result. Which means they must feel good about it, one and all! And that, of course, is never possible.

> Others: "Well, sure, *they* like it. After all, they're
>   his friends. But it certainly does nothing for
>   me!"

• And, finally, you should recognize that there is no way in the world to accurately pre-test a decision before the fact. Trial balloons are notorious liars. Ask any politician.

> You: "But, sir, I asked you about this before I
> did it. I had your okay."

> Boss: "Not for this you didn't!"

No wonder many clinical psychologists believe that successful decision-making is more a matter of luck than of intelligence! And you know what kind of luck you always have!

Now, even if all of the above could somehow be discounted, there is still this cardinal rule of business life to consider: *It is the executives who judge decisions — not the men and women who make them — who are the true leaders of our corporate society.*

Think about that for a minute!

So why take a chance? Make up your mind, here and now, before you've turned another page: The sure way, the safe way, the foolproof way to the top rung of any corporate ladder is to never make a decision! Dodge #9.

We are perfectly aware that this thesis runs counter to all those true-blue, rags to riches, Horatio Alger bromides about initiative and pluck that most Boy Scouts and Girl Scouts were brought up on. These sterling character traits may well have fitted the facts of business life once, but no longer. All they can do for you today is to get you in trouble. Sincere mediocrity, studied equivocation and the ability to walk boldly sideways will take you much further in today's corporate world.[*]

---

[*] So far, these necessary talents have not been incorporated into the curriculum at the Harvard Business School. We predict they soon will be.

This is not to say that the distinguished, white-haired gentlemen who made those stirring convocation speeches when you and I graduated from college were wrong. They meant well. They were simply behind the times. The truths of their youth had turned into myths when they weren't looking.

In days of yore, the successful entrepreneur was, in fact, the decisive, square-jawed captain of industry you have always heard he was. He'd listen to his advisors (or not, as he chose), make up his own tough mind and, chin out and shoulders hunched forward, he'd power his way from one fortune to the next. He really made decisions, and let the chips (and the nay-sayers) fall where they may. If he failed, he'd take his lumps and start all over again. If he succeeded, he'd buy whatever he needed (including as many congressmen as required) to insure his next success.

Unlike today's generation of business managers, the old-time entrepreneur would start his own business by inventing something in his basement, bathtub or carriage house. "Eureka! I've found it!" he'd cry as the barn exploded and a new industry was born. Or he'd simply steal an idea from some wimpy Bob Cratchett who worked for him, or from some indigent inventor:

> Entrepreneur: "I don't see much future in your idea for a printing machine, Mr. Gutenberg, but I'll give you five guilders for it, so you can feed your family."

These old-style entrepreneurs—the John Rockefellers, Jay Goulds and Andrew Carnegies of the late 19th century—owned their own operations, lock, stock (51%) and patents. They paid for any required improvements out of their own pockets—or with whatever funds they could con out of widows, orphans and fathers-in-law.

Bless them—they made America!

But things are much tougher today. Now it takes huge chunks of borrowed capital to start an enterprise. That means dealing with stockholders, the SEC, the FTC and legions of independent auditors. The whole nine yards. None of these are as easy to buy off or push around as widows and orphans were in the good old days. Today's venture capitalist wants his money back next week—with lots of profit. And he wants to keep an eye on his money while you are using it. The men who operate today's big businesses aren't owners. They are managers. Hired hands. They are all expendable. And they're all being watched. Closely.

In olden, golden days, if the man who owned the business was daring enough to re-style his merchandise every ten years, or advertise on barn roofs, or move his factory to Bald Knob, Arkansas, it was no big deal. He could do it all for about $104.95.

But in the more expensive world of commerce we live in today, it costs millions simply to change one word on a cereal box, or to put a few commercials on a mildly successful sitcom. For that matter, it can cost a few mil just to put up a tin storage shack out back of the plant to keep your surplus widgets in. Which is why the slightest miscalculation can bring a rumbling avalanche of chaos, a storm of calumny, a tempest of corporate distemper, down on the head of the poor unfortunate who made the decision to start all that calculating in the first place. And, never forget, it brings poverty, too.

With stakes so enormous, why gamble?

Some readers may feel that the new risk-management software programs being beta tested in Silicon Valley will insure that any computer-driven decision we may feel bold enough to make will be absolutely correct. These programs will do so, we hope, by replacing human frailty with cold, digital logic. At the same time, we expect they will also insulate the man or woman at the keyboard from blame should the computer miscalculate.

Not so, unhappily. In the first place, as we have pointed out, the rightness or wrongness of any decision we make is not determined by logic. It is determined, instead, by a complex of factors so overwhelming in number and subtlety that even the fastest and most sophisticated Pentium-based computer would boggle its motherboard trying to handle them all.

Computers are logical, but decisions are not.

Secondly, computers have a reputation for infallibility. You can't shift the responsibility for a bad decision onto a computer because no one will ever believe that a computer could make so egregious an error. Garbage in, garbage out. Only humans can err, not IBMs, Dells or Gateways. So, if a bad decision is made via your computer, the blame must be yours!

Finally, since computers are so reliable and you are not, any attempt to transfer responsibility from yourself to the machine may result in your whole job being transferred to the computer. Since these devices are already doing most of your work, there is nothing left for you to do but take blame. If you can't do that, who needs you? It is obviously easier to unplug you than it is to unplug the computer!

As you can see, a computer does not reduce the hazards of making decisions; it actually increases them. You are, when you operate a computer, not only responsible for your own follies, but for those of a million or more microprocessors that don't give a damn about you!

Now we both know that you, of all people, were certainly born to be a decision-making leader, a steely-eyed, clear-thinking captain of industry, an empire-building capitalist in the old and honorable tradition. But let us also accept the sad fact that you were born a couple of generations too late. Unless you really expect to turn into the Jay Gould, Cornelius Vanderbilt, Thomas Edison, or John

Rockefeller of your generation, you must carefully cultivate the talent not to make decisions. Because, in the here and now (as we hope we have convinced you), getting to the top isn't a matter of being smart enough to make the right decisions about business matters. It is, instead, a matter of being smart enough to make no decisions at all. It's a matter of being smart enough to avoid getting anything pinned on you.

The name of the game is responsibility-evasion! The crafty application of Dodge #9.

It's easy to make the decision to make no decisions. But it's very hard to actually carry out that resolve. In the pages that follow we offer a compendium of decision-situations that you will surely face in the year 2001 and beyond, and strategies for dealing with each of them. In this way, we will teach you how to keep from sinking into the doom that otherwise awaits.

Chapter Four

Let the Decision Make Itself

How to Look the Other Way

The first rule of responsibility-evasion is the simplest to state, but the hardest to live up to. It is this: when faced with a decision, *do nothing at all!*

Let the decision make itself.

When first confronted with a situation that appears to demand an immediate decision in order to avert a crashing disaster, the business neophyte churns into action at once. Casting caution to the wind, he or she makes a precipitous decision. Perhaps even two or three! And, even worse, the decision-maker actually enjoys it! There is a glow of inner satisfaction. A halo appears to hover overhead. The decision-maker savors the heady exhilaration that comes with a sense of command, sees himself or herself in the spotlight of glory, earning immediate field promotion to the topmost echelons of the company as a reward for quick, decisive action under pressure and amid panic.

But the decision-maker soon learns that the decision, whatever it was, was a mistake and the dreams a lie. For, in the normal course of events, the crisis will eventually pass. That's the way it is with crises. They usually just go away all by themselves.

But most young people don't know that. They think that they must *do* something. They don't realize that the decision-person becomes the responsible person and thus, by definition, the vulnerable person. After a short while, nobody remembers the special circumstances that made an immediate decision imperative—not even the decision-maker himself. The only things anyone remembers afterwards are the things that went wrong. And, in a crisis, things *always* go wrong—as often as not, via a form of guilt by association: The person who made the decision that relieved the crisis is, in retrospect, *blamed* for the crisis itself.

You can't win.

The better way is to do nothing at all. Apply Dodge #9. Rest assured that, when a decision is required and nobody is foolhardy enough to make it, the problem will go away all by itself. Or the momentum of events will make its own choice with no help from you. The decision will simply make itself; by gravity, by osmosis, by magic, by default. The laws of chance will go into effect—which simply means that the decision that makes itself has at least a fifty-fifty shot at being correct. Those are considerably better odds than you would have if you made the decision.

Please note that the world is awash in useless deci-sions—decisions that never had to be made in the first place. After forty-five years of observation, this student of corporate dynamics has concluded that at least 80% of all man-made decisions were totally unnecessary in the first place, and that the situations that gave rise to them would have resolved themselves just as satisfactorily had no overt decision to solve them been made at all!

The lesson to be drawn is this: Always allow nature to take its course with as little help from you as possible. There is nothing as inexorable as nature. And nothing with a better won-lost record. Who are you to fight Mother Nature?

With these facts so self-evident to any observer, why is it that people are so eager to make decisions at every opportunity? The fault lies in our childhood training. We were all brought up to live and act in a world that no longer exists. From the moment of birth, we are force-fed, along with our Enfamil, the philosophy that every person's destiny is in his or her own hands, if that person will but be decisive; grasp the nettle, join the fray, throw full weight, commit fully.

This is foolishness. Destiny belongs to no man or woman. Only the dull-witted delude themselves into thinking otherwise. Destiny is fate and *fate is blind luck* – and a better decision-maker than you'll ever be.

The evidence is all around you, in big things and small. Decide in advance where you want to take an important client for lunch next week, have your secretary make the reservations days in advance, and, chances are, when the day and time arrives, you'll wait thirty minutes for your table and the food will be lousy. Your client will give his business to your worst competitor.

On the other hand, just accidentally happen into a smart restaurant with your customer, and you'll be seated at once, dine like a king, and the stranger at the next table will pick up your tab just because he likes the cut of your jib. Your client will double his order for your widgets.

Or make a carefully considered decision to market a new product after years of research and development, and three competitors will have an improved version of your big idea on the market before you've even finished re-tooling. But let someone down on the production line accidentally create a new product by mistake (like Post-it Notes), and you'll find you have a five-year lead on the competition and that customers are spilling in over the transom to buy up all you can make. It happens more often than you realize!

Think back for a moment about the last half-dozen decisions you have been foolish enough to make, before you ever heard of Dodge #9. Can you honestly say, in retrospect, that they were really necessary? Any of them? Or that they actually improved the situation they were designed to improve? Of course not! Yet, remember the agony you went through as you weighed all the factors, considered all the ramifications, gathered all the data before making up your mind. It wasn't worth it, was it?

And now, try to remember the last time the CEO of your company made a decision. You can't, can you? He already knows about Dodge #9. That's why he is up there and you are still down here.

The fact is that, just as nature abhors a vacuum, man's nature abhors decisions. As more than one researcher has pointed out, man's natural inclination is to avoid "the agony of choice." Our basic natures, you see, try to save us. But our teachers deceived us. They taught us to feel morally duty-bound to solve problems by making decisions. The experience is, unfortunately, addictive. We grow to like the feeling of power it gives us. We come to believe that it is, somehow, intrinsically better to be a decisive failure than a spineless success.

Of course, letting decisions make themselves takes a lot of spine. It is not an easy matter. It is an art. When a crisis comes along that appears to require an immediate decision, everything conspires against us. Our moral teaching sets up an inner turmoil. An urgent clamor for action arises from colleagues on all sides. A person must be strong, indeed, to resist the urgent pressure to "do something."

If you are a novice at letting decisions make themselves, here are nine pointers that will help you stay ahead of the game during difficult, decision-demanding days:

1. When people around you hysterically cry out for action, try to give the impression that you are just on the verge of making a decision, even though you really have no intention of doing so. This, in itself, will do much to calm your associates. If you let them suspect

that a decision is not immediately in the offing, all manner of lamentation will ensue.

Instead, keep a sheaf of crumpled papers clutched in your hand and dash through the office corridors frequently with a tight smile on your face, stopping now and then to murmur "chin up" to whoever is standing around the office microwave. Keep your office door closed for long periods; you can use the naptime. Have your wife's idiot cousin come to visit you, but pretend that he is an outside consultant. This will reassure everyone.

> You: "We're working on it folks. Go back to
> your cubicles. Chin up!"

2. Reduce speed. Learn to waste time profitably. For starters, be the last one in your organization to appear to recognize that an urgent decision-situation has arisen. Move slowly. Pause often for desultory conversations. Laugh it up. Take long lunches. If you go to lunch with office people, say,

> "Now, for once, fellows, let's not talk business.
> Bad for the digestion, you know. Ha-ha!"

People will begin to think that matters aren't as urgent as they thought, and that you, perhaps, know something they don't.

3. Be terribly busy elsewhere so that the decision-situation can't catch up with you. Take a field trip. Get out to the West (or East) coast. Go after a new account in London or Paris. Have long, solitary, do-not-disturb conferences with your pretty (or handsome) secretary. Have your prostate or ovaries removed. Catch a cold. But, no matter what, be too busy to pay any attention at all to whatever it is that people think you ought to be paying attention to.

> You: "I'm too tied-up right now, folks. But I'll
> get to it in a couple of weeks. That's a prom-
> ise."

4. When you can no longer conveniently ignore the situation, LEAP into action with intense fury. Appoint a group to study the situation and instruct them, urgently, to report back to you in 60 or 90 days. If you can manage it, stack the committee against itself by...

a. Appointing people manifestly unqualified to discuss the matter at hand:

> "Yes, I know Mary is just a typist, but I'd like
> her opinion on restructuring our fiscal poli-
> cies."

b. Selecting people of sharply divergent views and personalities, and conflicting or competitive career aspirations, or choose the most blatant male chauvinists to work with the most ardent feminists in the company.

> "Now Jack and Jill, I know that you don't
> always agree on things, but I'd like you to
> pull together for the good of the company."

Such clever stacking of the committee will almost certainly result in both majority and a minority report, thus requiring that you...

5. Appoint another committee to study the first committee's report and suggest a compromise course of action. That will take another 60 to 90 days.

6. When all the reports are finally in, have a large staff meeting to discuss and consider them. This may require breaking the group down into subcommittees. Which means that nothing at all will get done at the first meeting.

7. Better have another meeting.

8. And another.

9. Repeat the first eight steps.

If, after all this, nature hasn't taken her course and made your decision for you, please don't feel that you must do something rash. Sometimes decisions are bashful and don't want to make themselves. But there are still other ways to evade responsibility and its evil consequences. Read on.

If you need something more to stiffen your spine, just imagine trying to manage your expensive lifestyle on unemployment checks.

Evading Responsibility to the Bitter End

Marvin L., the eldest but least talented of the sons of a retailing genius, eventually inherited management of his father's retail chain after the wise old man passed away. Marvin quickly realized, when he became Chairman, that he didn't have the smarts to run a cash register, let alone a large multi-store chain. So he looked for stand-ins who would make the important decisions for him.

Marvin turned first to stand-in Number One, the tall, handsome and well-spoken president of one of his chain's subsidiaries. This man dressed well, could charm the gold watch fob off a banker's vest, yet didn't know what the hell he was doing much of the time. He made the decision, with Marvin's thankful blessing, to borrow heavily to fund his division's Christmas business one November. But he ordered too late and the merchandise never arrived for the holiday season. Business was bad, so he couldn't pay for the merchandise when it did arrive, the following January. The failure of this one division, to Marvin's dismay, drove the whole company into Chapter 11. The handsome guy left with bonuses.

To rescue the company from bankruptcy, Marvin then hired another handsome executive to become President/CEO of the chain and to take over responsibility for deciding what to do. But, while pretending to save the company, the new chief executive shrank the firm to a third of its previous size, moved its offices to Arizona (where he liked the weather), looted its coffers and then managed to step aside just as the company teetered on the edge of final ruin.

In one last brilliant effort, just as the company was slipping below the waves, Marvin managed to sell off his father's stores to another retailer, who bought them for their real estate.

However, since he was already head man of his company, Marvin didn't suffer the fate that less senior executives with his dismal track record would have suffered. He still had some of daddy's millions and he took them to Arizona where he sits on the boards of several charities and at least one art museum.

Some people have all the luck.

Chapter Five

Let America Decide for You

Using Polls to Evade Responsibility

The next best thing to nobody is everybody. If a decision simply refuses to make itself, let all America do it for you!

How can you make 290 million Americans responsible for your decision? Just as they do it in politics — through the creative use of opinion polls. These days, everything else is done by polls, including the election of presidents. Why not make decisions that way, too? The way candidates and congressmen do.

Simply call in your research department and have them conduct a survey to find out what America thinks the right decision ought to be. The results of the survey become your decision. And a safe one, at that. Anyone who carps about a decision made by over 290 million Americans is certainly not a patriot.

To illustrate this technique, let's take a completely imaginary example and develop it step by step. Let's imagine that you are a departmental automotive executive who has been asked to make a decision as to whether your Detroit company should, or should not, begin production of a new line of sports utility vehicles that use less gasoline to achieve high mileage, and which can leap over small streams and carry up to fourteen adults.

The first step, since you obviously don't want to be held personally responsible for so earth-shaking a decision, would be to go out and hire yourself a research firm. There are thousands to choose from. Or turn the problem over to your company's own internal research department.

In any case, the research folks will mull over the problem for awhile, in order to enhance their feeling of self-importance. Then they will submit a Plan. The Plan will consist of a Methodology (the form they believe the research should take), a Questionnaire (what they intend to ask people in order to get answers, and please note that the questionnaire may or may not have questions related to SUVs), and a Sample (a description of the people whose responses, you are assured, will be representative of the responses of all the people in America whose opinions you seek). The sample doesn't have to be large; a clever clutch of researchers can make a dozen people sound like the Mormon Tabernacle Choir, statistically speaking.

Having done all this, and perhaps after conducting a pilot test or two among their wives, husbands and significant others, the opinion researchers will venture out into the world (via the telephone, of course — nobody ever talks face-to-face anymore) and ask their questions of America, or as much of America as they believe necessary. In two or three months, they will return with the Answer — a thick, chart-choked document spilling over with tabulations, tables, graphs, computer printouts and thoughtfully hedged executive summaries.

After careful study, and many, many meetings, all concerned will agree that the report definitely proves that American automobile buyers care nothing about buying sports utility vehicles — no matter what gut feelings to the contrary some people may have. You can scrap the plans for a gas-efficient SUV. Let those dumb folks at Suzuki do it!

The beauty of it is that this really isn't your decision at all. You can never be held responsible for it. Nobody can pin anything on you. The decision is America's decision — which you will simply administer! You are thus in a perfect position to claim credit for all of the good things that may flow from the decision, such as the millions the firm will save by not re-tooling its plants. But you can never be blamed for any of the bad effects that may arise from the decision, such as a severe case of Chapter Eleven.

If, in a few years, when every other vehicle on the road is an SUV, the fact that your firm missed the boat cannot be blamed on you. The blame belongs to all Americans, whose duplicity when answering questions is well known to research people and income tax folk alike. So you, if not your company, are safe. And that's what it's all about!

Because of its great usefulness as a tool in the art of responsibility-evasion (rather than for any useful facts it might accidentally happen to discover), research has been one of America's fastest growing industries in the past couple of decades.[*] Any company worth its plush executive suites gets a research director almost as soon as it gets its stationery. And independent research companies have proliferated as rapidly as rabbits, and in somewhat the same manner. It is estimated that, in a very few years, your fingers will have to walk twice as far as they do now to cover all the research firms listed in the Yellow Pages.

Advertising is a good example of an industry that relies heavily on research to avoid corporate and personal responsibility for some of the silly campaigns they sell their clients. Soap companies, along with political candidates

---

[*]   Think tanks are a growing industry, too. They are much like research companies except that people in think tanks are a lot smarter and generally feel qualified to have opinion without benefit of statistical support. But it is dangerous to base an opinion on anything a genius tells you. If your genius is so smart, why the hell isn't he in politics, where the big money is?

and automobile makers, are today's primary consumers of research, engulfing themselves constantly in thoughtful and innovation-choking waves of data about every conceivable aspect of American opinion. What these people and their research suppliers don't know about America is hardly worth knowing. In fact, a good deal of what they *do* know is hardly worth knowing!

Advertising agencies do research on client products to see if they're any good. (They always are.) Motion picture companies do research to see why people won't go to see their movies. (People don't think they're so good). Others research violence in movies, sex in music, prurient thought in novels. They find what they're looking for wherever they look. Great! It is reported that some corporate executives won't even go to a three-martini lunch until their research department assures them it's noon. And for good reason.

Things have changed in the world of business. Once upon a time, as we have indicated, industry was run by bull-headed entrepreneurs. These were men (and occasional women) who had the gift of persuasion and a gut feeling about what people were likely to want. And they were willing to spend money making it. They didn't need research. The companies these people ran were extensions of their own personas.

Most of these industrial leaders knew exactly how to sell what they made. When one of them had an advertising idea, he'd draw it up on the back of a cocktail napkin and run it in a magazine. It didn't cost an awful lot. So, if the magazine ad wasn't very effective, he didn't get terribly mad about it. Overall, the batting average of these old pros was no worse—maybe a little better—than the average that big-time ad agencies achieve today. And it didn't take a huge research project to find out.

But today's businesses have consolidated, merged and re-merged to become very large and institutionalized. And very cautious. The old masters are a dying breed. They're mostly all gone by now, or sitting with palsied hands in high, impotent offices, wondering at what they've wrought.

Many of today's corporations are huge, impersonal institutions with thousands of narrowly specialized employees and acres of esoteric departments, divisions and services. Producing and marketing their products is a hugely expensive undertaking. The cost of placing advertising for those products before the public is literally astronomical. One thirty second spot on a highly rated show can cost more than the average Joe makes in a lifetime. A year-long advertising budget can cost hundreds of millions of dollars. Coca-Cola's ad budget could fund Belgium.

In short, the stakes have become so high, in both cold cash and in human terms as well, that only a dedicated masochist would put his own neck on the block by gambling on his own judgment to make a business decision about anything. With so many millions of dollars riding on it, something will always go wrong. It's bound to happen. But why should you be the fall guy? Why risk your career when you can lean on—and hide behind—the combined judgment of millions of people? That's why research was invented.

If you're in the movie business, the lawyer business, the retail business, the construction business, the publishing business, or any other business, if your customer doesn't like what you've done for him, you can use research to prove how wrong he is. When you have a research report in hand, you can always cite the fact that 74% of all respondents (aided and unaided recall) liked whatever the client hated and rated it "above average." No matter what he really thinks, no executive has gumption enough to go up against 74% of the American people without having some serious second thoughts.

Further, if it turns out that the product and/or service that your client didn't like really was, in fact, a bomb, you are still in the clear. After all, it was all America, or at least 74% of Americans, that misled you. Or was it your research director who misled you by misreading research results? (Which is why internal research directors always call in outside research companies to do the slippery work. They know about Dodge #9, too.)

No matter what business your company is in, the technique still works. Make no mistake, research is a tremendously effective way to evade decision responsibility. But, if you're new at playing the research game, here are a few things you should know:

1. Don't get all het up over whether the research is accurate or not. There is a vast difference between validity and usefulness—and the latter is all you are interested in. As for validity, keep in mind that even the most carefully conducted research has a sometimes substantial margin of error. It isn't always right. There are some critics who question whether it is ever right. This may be an extreme view.

Yet, when you look at all the bad movies, books, fashions, and dog food ads on television, on the Internet, or in your mailbox, and realize that it has all been researched to hell and gone, you can understand the critic's suspicions. The cult of research has grown far more rapidly than the art of research. The point you want to remember is that you need not be concerned with the accuracy of the research. You aren't, after all, looking for truth. Responsibility-evasion is your goal. Dodge #9. Everything else is lagniappe.

2. The second important thing to know is that, through careful study and the gingerly weighting of results, any piece of research can be legitimately interpreted to support any position you care to take.

In a recent TV commercial, a hired "personality" told viewers that 45% of people tested liked a certain popular brand of coffee, so it must be good. Left unsaid was the easily deduced conclusion that 55% of respondents thought the stuff was not so good. So, while you may not want to take a public position on any decision made via research (indeed, it would be most unwise to do so), the proper interpretation of even the most contrary findings can help you exercise any privately-held predilection you may have.

> "Obviously," you may say in a meeting to discuss research results, "there are subliminal, non-verbal factors at work here and these must be taken into account when judging the results of this study. Thus, when properly weighted in this way, the 3% favorable response actually equates to a total of 81% favorable. Ladies and gentlemen, our course is clear!"

No one will understand what it is you've said, but all will happily accept the conclusion. As long as they are not responsible for it.

3. You should also know that research data can be skewed your way before the fact—if you happen to be in a position of enough authority in your firm to exercise life-and-death influence over the corporate careers of your research people. You need not, therefore, remain helpless on the sidelines while waiting for research results.

A simple discussion before the data is reported may have an important effect on the thinking of the research people involved. In this way, the figures and charts produced by the team working on your problem can be shown to prove precisely whatever it is you would like them to prove. Unpleasant surprises can thus be avoided. For example:

> You (to the research director): "Wouldn't be surprised, Nancy, if you discovered that the yellow and brown package was the best liked ... just as I always suspected."
>
> Nancy: "Well—ah—sure. I've always been on your side in that matter, sir."
>
> You: "You're my gal, Nancy!"
>
> Nancy: "Don't I know it!"

This is not really cheating, per se. Given the feeble record of most "research" in finding answers to important questions, your "help" may actually help. It certainly isn't going to hurt.

4. There are all kinds of research. Some are a simple matter of counting noses, directly questioning respondents and adding up of their answers. Others can be deeply Freudian probes of the psyches of respondents.

You can always tell which is which because the questionnaires used in the latter tend to contain phrases like "phallic symbolism," "penis envy," "Oedipus complex" or the word "syndrome," in their summaries. Especially "syndrome."

The kind of research you should choose depends not on the kind of information you want to get but on the personality of the person you want to convince. If he or she is a sales manager, for example, simple nose counting is fine. If he is an executive who inherited the business from his father (whom he therefore hates), or one who has undergone psychotherapy, the deep stuff is what you want. You can then begin your presentation with the words, "psychologically speaking," and he or she will buy anything that follows.

5. The number of respondents in the sample is not important. The research department will want to start with a cast of thousands, but twenty or thirty will usually be sufficient for your purpose. After all, Nielsen is reported to use just two television homes in Billings, Montana, to project the viewing habits of the whole damned state. However, if you use relatively few respondents, be sure to make all the charts reflect percentages. "96% of all respondents stated that..." will sound a whole lot better to the person you are trying to convince than "Eight people said...."

6. Learn some research argot so that, without sounding too ridiculous, you can pull off phrases like, "Based on a bi-polar attitudinal survey ... blah ... blah ... blah. It is obvious that what America is looking for is "blah ... blah ... blah." Or, "A statistically significant sample, based on all available demographic data, would seem to indicate ... blah ... blah ... blah." Such language will add luster to your image inside of your firm as well as outside of it. You don't have to know what the words mean. No one ever does.

7. No matter how thin the data, research reports themselves must always be thick. Two inches is a good hefty average. You can accomplish this by having everything charted, including the title page, when the report is being bound together at the copy machine. And you can toss in any extra statistical tables left over from earlier surveys that you may happen to have lying around the office. Your objective is to keep people from reading anything but the executive summary of conclusions and recommendations, the content of which you may be able to influence more easily.

"Ladies and gentlemen," you will say, "let's not
take the time now to go through all the
charts and tables — you can do that later.
Let's turn, instead, directly to the summary
section that begins on page 971."

No one, of course, will ever give the charts and tables a second glance.

So much for research. You will find it a most effective way to have decisions made without your direct involvement. Wisely used, it can relieve you of the onus of decision-responsibility while still leaving decision-authority firmly in your hands.

Remember, you can be forced into early retirement for a wrong decision. But nobody can force 74% of America into early retirement.

Every thinking businessman is aware that America's population is aging rapidly. As baby boomers begin to reach their retirement years, many seek to cater to them, to woo their loyalty. Democrats seek votes by swearing allegiance to Social Security and Medicare. Republicans try to win them over by eliminating estate taxes and cutting capital gains rates. And so on. No wonder. This generation of seniors is the most affluent, the healthiest and the longest-lived of any generation in history.

Some industries are going with this flow. Supermarkets stock more salt and sugar-free foods, but in hard to find sections in corner nooks and crannies. Restaurants offer senior specials but only from 4:30 till 6:00 p.m. Movies charge over-fifty folks cut rates at the box office.

But, surprisingly, the business world at large is not doing very well by seniors. Why, for example, are most movies these days aimed at youngsters? (Star Wars, American Pie, etc.) Why are there so many sitcoms aimed at sub-thirty viewers? (Moesha, Sabrina the Teenage Witch, Buffy the Vampire Slayer, etc., to say nothing of MTV.) Why do so many TV commercials set their sights on young adults when it is old adults who control most of the disposable income in the new century—and who will control even more every year for the next twenty?

If you've been paying attention thus far, you will realize that all this is because the people in charge of making age-related decisions in entertainment, apparel, retailing, electronics, etc., are up to their ears in Dodge #9. They are avoiding their responsibilities because they know that, sure as tomorrow and taxes, that if they make a decision, they will lose: lose face, lose seniority, lose the decision. And lose their chance at a top spot in their company.

So they eagerly delegate these decisions to underlings. However, the only underlings brash enough to make them are idiot youngsters who haven't yet discovered the importance of Dodge #9. Being young, these fledgling subordinates cast their votes for what will please them, not what may appeal to the folks who have the money to buy the sponsor's product and the free time to use it. So when these ambitious subordinates choose "Harriet, the

High School Harlot" for a prime-time network slot and it turns out to be a bomb (as it most certainly will), young heads will roll and grayer wiser heads will shake with guiltless disapproval. Some executives can use up a whole army of ambitious young Harvard MBAs while making their own ways up the ladder of success. But, after all, isn't that what MBAs are for?

Chapter Six

Hiding in the Hierarchy

Playing Hide & Seek with Decision

The art of responsibility-evasion is not simply a matter of adroitly passing the buck, it is a matter of never letting the buck get anywhere near you. This brings us to a consideration of the organizational structure of the typical corporation, and of how you can use that structure to sidetrack any buck that seems to be heading your way.

There are a few exalted positions in the hierarchy of the typical American corporation whose occupants are, traditionally and by definition, well insulated from the dangers of decision-making. They are:

1. The Chairman of the Board.

    Whatever he does is, by definition, right.

2. The son or daughter (or son-in-law or daughter-in-law) of the Chairman.

    "Love me, love my kids."

3. Any independent consultant hired to look in on the corporation. (As long as he doesn't have anything negative to say).

    "I want to thank you for giving me this opportunity...."

4. A favored member of the headquarters junta who acts as sort of an intellectual corporate jester. Often this is a college professor who was accidentally recruited along with some of his graduate students and who deals only in well-qualified opinions and abstract analyses that nobody understands. He is used to point to with pride.

"Thank you, Professor, for your keen insight."

If, however, you are not a member of any of these carefree breeds, there are still ways to achieve, by clever manipulation, what they have achieved through occupational heredity or blind good fortune.

You must first learn to manipulate and exploit the basic organizational set-up of your company. You must wedge yourself into a flow chart of your organization that assures that nothing of importance ever flows your way. If your company is like most, you will find its structural confusion a great help to you as you set out to avoid responsibility.

Most companies, as you have surely noted, are organized not to facilitate action, but to frustrate it. On paper, these corporate organizational charts are artistically symmetrical arrangements of people and official titles, boxed and charted in a manner that is intended to satisfy mankind's inherent yearning for balance and beauty. Neatness counts. But in actuality, as any organization man or woman soon learns, most businesses are a rat's nest of twisting channels, tortuous procedures, frozen processes, hidden agendas and fragmented responsibilities, all haphazardly Scotch-taped together in a way that makes the orderly flow of business as disorderly as possible without cutting it off altogether.

Many organizational structures are masterpieces of obfuscatory administrative architecture in the Far Side tradition. They surpass the late Rube Goldberg's fondest nightmares. To wit:

1. Titles don't describe function. Thus responsibility is not traceable. The Public Relations VP may head up the mailroom. The Communications Director can be the kid who types out the company newsletter. The title Chief of Production may indicate the guy who orders software for the IBMs. And so on.

2. Lines of real authority don't necessarily follow the lines of authority as specified on the organization chart, but instead snake their way secretly and without discernible pattern throughout the organization. Tracing them is like trying to unravel a bowl of spaghetti — and just as slippery.

3. There are a great many decision levels from top to bottom: The more advanced the company is organizationally, the more decision levels there are. Yet there is no single focus of responsibility at any level.

Several people are required to make every decision on every level — and usually fight among themselves to do so. The winner takes all: blame.

While a multitude of decision levels in a company mitigate against its rational operation, it also makes it less possible to trace root responsibility. The advantages, you see, outweigh the disadvantages.

But the real works of art in organizational architecture go far beyond this. By making a careful study of your own organization's structure, and contriving a few, slightly noticeable alterations, you may be able to create an organizational chart so wondrously convoluted that your own responsibility for decision-making is forever concealed in a forest of squares, boxes and dotted lines.

It is, in fact, possible to create an organizational hierarchy in which no one reports to you and you report to no one! (See Chart #602 on p. 54.) You are thus free to call policy meetings, write demanding and even insulting memos and make frequent tours of inspection to London, Paris,

Rome and the Greek Islands — and yet be completely free of responsibility to anyone for anything.

Of course, unless you are quite senior in the organization, such masterful alterations may be difficult to pull off. However, a thoughtful study of your organizational chart will probably show you several almost-as-effective ways to shunt responsibility onto other tracks whenever it starts highballing your way.

Such a study might show you, for example, which other divisions in the company could conceivably be manipulated into the target area by a clever appeal to management:

> You: "I think Dave's group would be much better at handling the Crinch matter, Boss, since they have so much more experience in that sort of thing than my group does."

An examination of your company's organization chart may also show you ways in which slight changes in procedural routines can remove you from areas of potential responsibility before they occur. For example, a memo to the division chief with an ingenuous suggestion:

> You: "By having specifications sent directly through Charlie's group, rather than through our bunch here — as now shown on the division flow chart — things can be moved along more quickly and free my staff so that they can do their jobs with greater efficiency."

This may work even if receiving specifications is your group's sole function. And it may earn you the monthly cash award for making the company's Suggestion Incentive program appear to be working.*

---

* So few people put anything at all into the Suggestion Box at most companies that almost any idiotic proposal stands a good chance of being rewarded. The only requirement is that it sound vaguely sincere, no matter how stupid it really is.

The structure of the hierarchy of your company, as we have shown, offers many ways for you to successfully evade responsibility for making any decisions whatsoever. Study that structure. There's a life of ease and security hidden somewhere in that maze. If you can only find it.

Typical Corporate Organizational Chart

(Chart #602) Altered to Protect the Innocent

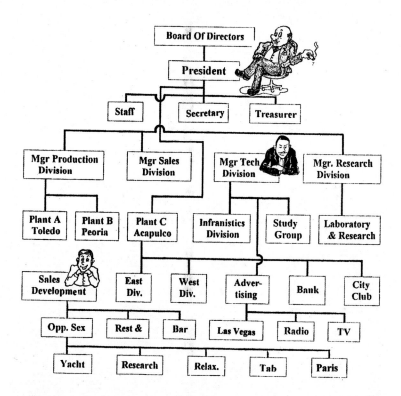

NOTES TO CHART: You can easily see how the president of this organization has managed to handle his awesome responsibilities. He is able to keep as busy as he wants to be kept—and no busier. But also notice how two other executives on the chart have been able to arrange comfortable careers with the aid of the company's official organization chartist. The manager of the Tech Division—a department no one has ever bothered to define—has an interesting set of job responsibilities which often keep him working long after hours. And, even lower in the hierarchy, note how the person in charge of sales development has managed to keep himself completely free of any encumbering responsibilities at all.

The Boss Who Made a Mistake

Hans X. was the Chairman of the Board of a famous Milwaukee beer.

He was a handsome man even into his late seventies, who wore caps and capes and drove a convertible when he wasn't being chauffeured. Because his family owned the brewery, and he headed the family, Ike ran the company as a personal fiefdom. He decided everything. But usually he was smart enough to rely on the advice of his staff before making the most important decisions.

However, a time came when he didn't consult his staff for their input. Ike decided to launch a second lower-tier brand of beer to go with his top-of-the-line brand. He asked the Board of Directors for permission to get the new brew brand started and was turned down flat. Too expensive, they said. Too chancy. But Mr. X. was not one to take orders from anyone. He decided that he would launch his new beer all by himself—secretly. So he couldn't ask his staff for advice and counsel.

He devised a wonderful advertising campaign for the new brew, and determined that he was going to have it bottled in green bottles with a bright red cap, rather than the usual brown glass bottles that all beers came in those days.

Finally, when everything was ready to go, Ike presented the product to his Board of Directors as a fait accompli. They accepted, reluctantly. The huge copper brewing pots began to manufacture the product, and pour it into miles of green bottles with bright red caps. The trucks backed up to the loading docks to express the beer to distributors across the country.

Then—disaster! Seems that the fluorescent lights in distributors' warehouses reacted negatively with the new (and never tested) green glass of the bottles—and when the caps were snapped, the contents were vinegar.

The message: Decision-makers should always have someone else make the important decisions! Even when they have already reached the top.

Chapter Seven

Create a Consensus

The Safety in Numbers

The higher you get on the ladder of success, the closer the danger of decision-making moves to your desk. And the more necessary it becomes that you remain cool, calm and resourceful.

The preferred method for handling — and avoiding — decision situations that may break through your outer defenses is to have the required decisions arrived at by what is known as a consensus; that is, having a large number of people produce, and concur in, the decision that must be made. In this sense, a consensus is indistinguishable from a compromise. It is, in fact, simply a group decision. The more people who participate, the thinner the coating of responsibility that gets painted on any one person in the group. Each is given "cover" by the crowd around him or her.

In fact, if you can create a broad enough base, the film of responsibility that sticks to you may be so thin as to be invisible. There is safety in numbers. Two may be company, but three (or more) is insurance.

"Consensus" is a holy word in the business world. And in government too, as recent presidents have taught us. It has the sacred ring of democracy about it, an echo of the business bromide that holds that two heads are better than one. Nobody can be against a consensus. It provides the wise executive with a wonderful escape route in his bobbing and weaving battle to implement Dodge #9 in his business career. He or she can thus never be caught making a mistake. It is this united front that masks responsibility. But there are a few things about the art of creating a consensus that every executive must clearly understand, if only to avoid deceiving himself or herself.

The first is that the word "consensus" is not a synonym for the word "correct." A decision reached and supported by a majority is not, by definition, the *right* decision, though it is fashionable to pretend that it is. There is, on the contrary, good reason to believe that there is a negative correlation between consensus and correctness. Fifty million Frenchmen were wrong, Edsel and DeLorean failed, Sony lost billions in the movie business, the Republicans nominate Al Damato for Senate, Sunbeam hired "Chainsaw Al"—and then had to fire him. You can name dozens more!

Although almost all major business decisions are today arrived at through the torturous achievement of a consensus within the organization concerned, more than half of these decisions turn out, in the end, to have been wrong. Example: For every three thousand new products considered for the market last year, fewer than three got into stores and only one managed to achieve even a modest level of success. The real triumphs were one in three thousand! But all three thousand products had the wholehearted support of the organizations that brought them to market.

However, even when you come to realize the almost unfailing failure of consensus, it is not considered cricket in the business world to let on that you are aware of it. It is one of those things that all smart people know in their gut but are too nice to mention.

A second thing to understand about the concept of consensus is why, if it is such a lousy way to arrive at decisions, so many business leaders demand it? In fact, it often appears that the higher a person has risen in an organization, the more he wants the security of a general agreement in support of his views (and the easier it is for that person to achieve it!). The answer to this question lies in the nature of the business hierarchy itself.

To grasp it, you must first open your eyes to the obvious fact that, with few exceptions, the topmost people in business are seldom qualified for the topmost jobs they hold. This is because the talents that business leaders (or political leaders, for that matter) must exercise to get to the top have virtually nothing to do with the talents they must exercise after they get there!*

Sales wizards must somehow become desk-bound administrators, introspective laboratory scientists must become after-dinner speakers, company accountants must become corporate statesmen. Imagine the storms of self-doubt, the castrating fears of inadequacy that must roil in those executive bellies! Only the security of consensus, the confident knowledge that the whole company stands behind him or her in admiring agreement, can relieve the anxiety that a modern CEO feels as he tries to do his job. Consensus is his Prozac and his Viagra. And the rest of the organization, taking its cues from the top, therefore demands consensus all down the line—thus astronomically compounding the chances for an ill-considered decision.

A third point to know: To be most effective, a consensus must cut the widest possible swath through the organiza-

---

* "Despite all personnel procedures, and perhaps because of them, superior performance at the apex of any organization is frequently, in the deepest sense, accidental." Who should know better than Henry Kissinger, who wrote this during his salad days as a Harvard professor long before he ever became a Secretary of State to Nixon, an elder statesman, and head of his own think tank. Henry A. Kissinger, *Education for Public Responsibility* (Norton, NY, 1961).

tion. The broader it is, the more suitable it is as a device for responsibility-evasion. Naturally, the extent of the support you can command is usually determined by your level in the corporate hierarchy, plus whatever incremental clout your good standing in the eyes of top management can additionally achieve. The higher you are, the broader the agreement you can command, since everyone who is your junior is, understandably, willing to agree with you rather than face dismissal. To put up with people who disagree with you weakens company discipline. Yes-men always do well, but there is no place for a no-man (or woman) in a well-run company.

You can always gauge a person's relative standing in a firm by counting the number of heads that nod reflexively in unison with his or hers at company meetings.

By definition, then, the president of a company can get almost instant agreement by consensus—and the widest possible dilution of responsibility—whenever he or she needs it.

At lower echelons, it is somewhat more difficult to get an agreement that extends beyond the sphere of your immediate influence, beyond the circle of subordinates whose bread and butter you already control. There are, however, certain techniques of consensus-expansion that you would do well to make use of whenever the need arises. For, unless you can build a base of support that is relatively broad, you may find the total weight of an unwelcome decision resting on your own narrow shoulders. Here are those techniques:

1. Attribute a point of view that you hold to a higher authority, perhaps the CEO, in order to achieve a consensus behind a decision. It is not important that the CEO actually holds the opinion you attribute to him—just that he can be *said* to hold it. The use of this technique is a little like playing a game of tag with responsibility. This dialog shows how it is done:

> You: "I hear the head honcho wants to do it this
>   way. What do you people think?"
>
> Joe: "I agree."
>
> Mary: "Same here."
>
> Jack: "I'm for that."
>
> You: "Well, okay then. If that's what you peo-
>   ple think."

Joe and his friends are now "it" and a consensus has
been achieved that will leave you blameless in case of
trouble.

2. Find a precedent. Prove that whatever it is that you
want to have done has already been done in other
places at other times, successfully. In this way, you may
be able to establish that a certain way of handling a
given situation is usual and customary. Therefore, no
decision is really required. What you intend to do is
S.O.P.—an accepted procedure under the present circumstances. You are merely the administrator of a
course of action that is a given, not the focus of responsibility. Consensus becomes almost automatic in such
circumstances. Like this:

> You: "As you are no doubt aware, this is exactly
>   the way that Wal-Mart, Ford Motors and
>   AT&T handled a similar situation back in
>   1984."
>
> All (with audible sigh of relief): "Hurrah! Hur-
>   rah!"

Incidentally, don't worry about the accuracy of the pre-
cedents you cite. Just reel off the names of a few companies now doing well on the Dow or Nasdaq in a self-
assured tone, plus a few dates (1984, a good year for

everything and remote enough to be uncheckable without a lot of research), and you are home free!

3. Shoehorn elements of everyone's thinking into an omnibus decision so that all concerned can feel pride in having contributed, and therefore all will own a share of the responsibility for it. Since a consensus is simply the activating clause of a decision, you can broaden it by broadening the base of the compromise behind it. If you are the one who constructs this camel, you can always make things move in the direction you choose without being too obvious about it.* The most junior member of the cabal so formed can usually be persuaded to present the group's decision to the management. He doesn't know the noose that dangles there!

4. Attribute your solution to your boss when you present it to him, and he will command the consensus you need for protection. This must be done carefully, to wit:

> You: "We're following the course of action you
> suggested, J. B. As usual, you were so right!"

Since executives say so much and forget most of what they say, your boss (1) will imagine that he actually did say something worthwhile, and (2) be awfully pleased that someone was paying attention to what he was saying, even if he wasn't.

A variation of this technique is to take something that your chief actually did say (usually in another context) and find a way to make it fit the decision you want made. Executives are often addicted to making deep, philosophic statements like "a straight line is the shortest distance between two points." Such a statement, for

---

* From that old saying, "A camel is an animal put together by consensus." There are lots of camels out there these days.

example, can become your authority to use the company plane for luxurious direct point-to-point field trips to replace the roundabout tourist class transportation you have been using.

5. Make collaborators out of your subordinates. When worse comes to worst, and the decision must be made right in your own bailiwick, gather your staff together and have them decide what you have already determined they ought to decide. True, this is a very limited consensus. But when you have a very limited area of discretion, it is best to make the most of what you have.

First, direct your subordinates to write a report along lines you suggest. They will be glad to comply in order to gain entry to the heady corporate level where (they think) the big perks are handed out. This report, prepared by innocent members of your staff, becomes the focus of responsibility. Use it as your authority.

6. From time to time, you will be called upon by others to become a supporter of a consensus. Chances are that, in the spirit of good sportsmanship, you will comply. However, it is wise in such circumstances to frame your support in such a way that an escape route remains open to you—should one be needed later. A few suggested phrases will illustrate the proper technique to use in such circumstances:

> You: "Sure, I'll go along if you want me to, but I'll have to take your word that you know what you're doing."

> or

> You: "Well, I don't really agree, but for the sake of preserving the peace (or moving ahead or getting this over with ... etc.), I'll go along with the majority."

or

You: "Okay, okay, okay! Who am I to stand in
the way of people who are so sure of themselves?"

If anything goes wrong later, you are in the clear! You
have Dodge #9 on your side.

Consensus, then, is the device to use when a decision-
situation takes point-blank aim at your career. While often
difficult to achieve, a consensus is still easier to find than a
new job. Even in these days when incompetents can get
jobs without really trying.

REALITY SNAPSHOT:
The Dot.Comedy

The Internet is where most business is going to be done a few years into the 2000s. Having a smart web site is crucial to any company that plans to be a success in the next few years. The test for any enterprise is to be WWW-literate.

Then why, you ask, do so many dot-com web pages start with a greeting from the chairman, the president or the CEO instead of a frank appeal for the sale? Why do so many home pages feature information about the company's stock before they talk about the company's products? And why do so many companies put their help-wanted appeals ahead of their selling appeals on the web?

Obviously, no company would begin a TV commercial with a corporate message from the president (unless you're Dave Thomas of Wendy's). You never see a Vogue magazine ad for diamonds from VanCleef and Arpels that also touts the stock of the company. And how often does a sleek ad for Lincoln Town Cars in the National Geographic begin with an appeal for new employees?

Yet these gaffes are routine on the Internet. The reason should be obvious. It's because the webmasters and designers who put together most Internet home pages are computer geeks, more interested in net play than in selling whatever it is that their companies make.

But somehow, even though they realize that the web sites they design are not what people on the Internet are really looking for, they do, somehow, know what their bosses are looking for: personal aggrandizement, increased value for their stock options and new employees to fill in for those who are terminated for making decisions.

Chapter Eight

Using Family & Friends to Get Out from Under

Helping Your Helpmate Help You

Family and friends are very useful when you are looking for someone to blame for your bad decision. Yes, we know that you owe allegiance and loyalty to those who are close to you. We know that your wife and children love you almost unconditionally, and are as anxious as you are that you achieve success, if only to keep you from kicking the dog.

But we also know that you can avoid being detected as an incompetent cipher by letting your wife, your husband, and/or your children participate in making needed decisions. And, when it turns out wrong—as it inevitably will—you can shift the blame to them. Don't worry; it will turn out okay.

All spouses/significant others want to help their helpmates become as successful as they always thought they would be some day. They always remember the "for richer" words of their wedding vows and forget the "for poorer" ones. And so spouses and children and significant others, as well as members of your extended family, are always anxious to support you in your quest for success.

It makes a spouse feel more secure in life if a husband or wife is secure in his/her job. So there is always high interest on the part of one to aid in the success of the other. After all, you'll need the other's salary if you lose your job.

Participating in a decision being made by a spouse can help cement a marriage. A husband or wife who discusses business with the other gives their partnership real meaning. Neither ever has to say, "Why don't you ever talk to me?"

Chances are, you've done it many times, but now you will be able to do it better.

> You: "Honey, I don't know what I'm going to do about overhauling our computers at the office. Old Grumpkin has tossed that hot potato in my lap and needs my decision on Tuesday. What do you think? Would it be wise, as I believe, to upgrade to new mainframes? Or just to go with what we have?"

Your spouse knows, of course, that Grumpkin is an ass—you've told her/him about that jerk a hundred times. So anything that Grumpkin wants is certain to be all wrong. And anything you say will, by process of elimination, be right. So...

> Spouse: "It's clear to me that you need those new mainframes. Sweetie, I'd just go and tell Grumkin that that's the way it's going to be, period."

Fine. You have your decision and a plausible "out" for later.

As a clever decision-avoider, you can get the same kind of help from your wife's bridge or exercise class, or your husband's poker and bowling buddies. These men and women are always eager to put their noses into your business, so give them a chance. Consider each such group an unofficial focus panel, and let them focus on your problem.

They'll love it. And they'll give you opinions that you can bend any way you see fit.

Same thing goes for your kids and their playmates. After they turn twelve, your kids already realize that you're a hopeless blowhard and will appreciate getting a word in edgewise. And, if they are actually asked for an opinion, they may mow the lawn out of gratitude. Kids. Who can figure?

So ask your son or daughter to check the youngsters at their school about favorite colors, sports stars, soft drink flavors, clothing styles, rap groups—and extrapolate from there. Since you are probably clueless about what the real solution to the problem is, it doesn't make much difference where you do your "research." Input from family and friends is as good as input from somebody else.

Please understand that you are not using family and friends because they actually have any information that bears on the decision you are trying to avoid. Accept the fact they will never provide you real solutions for the real problems you are trying to evade. How could your husband's golf buddies or your wife's Yoga class know enough to decide anything at all about your business? Same goes for your kids and their playmates.

But they can provide invaluable cover for a wrong decision, once you've made it.

The procedure is easy. First you must outline the problem you are trying to solve in as much detail as you think necessary. But not too much detail, please. Don't confuse anyone. You don't want informed answers; you just want baseless opinions you can use to buttress any decision you happen to tumble into.

Once you have dragooned your spouse, kids and their associates into offering an opinion, the next step is to announce the decision that flows from their input at the office. But while you are telling your superior what it is you have decided, it would be wise to also indicate that your position is the result of something more than just your gut feeling. Like research, for example.

> You: "Mr. Scruncher, I have done some unoffi-
> cial research among friends about that Inter-
> net problem you asked me to look into, and I
> have decided, based on that research, sir, to
> recommend that we get another Internet ser-
> vice provider."

> He: "Okay, kiddo, if you say that the research
> supports your conclusion, I'll go along with
> you for now."

As soon as you have put your company through the trauma of switching to another web service provider and it becomes clear that the whole operation has been a major folly and you are about to have your retirement pension cut from under you, you must figure out how to survive. Family and friends to the rescue!

No, family and friends won't make the bad decision become a good one. But they will afford you the cover you need when things begin to get ugly. You have to start bemoaning.

> You: "I should have used a better sample for my
> research. Then I'd have had the information
> I needed. Sorry, Mr. Flinche."

> He: "That's okay this time, young man (or
> woman), but don't let it happen again."

> You: "You can bet on it, sir."

Your superiors may be so impressed with the pains you took to reach your conclusion, even though it was wrong, that they will forgive the transgression without coming down too hard on you.

Or you can decide to be a tad more forthcoming about the thinking that went into your decision. If you are a man, do it like this:

> You: "I realized, when I got thinking about this problem, that my wife and her Yoga classmates had exactly the demographic profile we were seeking here. So I organized some focus groups — and took their answers. I realize now that no women with her ankles locked behind her head can think clearly. I promise that it won't happen again."

If you are a woman, your escape is essentially the same:

> You: "My husband is a very successful businessman whose company faced a very similar situation. So I enlisted him and several of his senior associates, both men and women, to help me come to my conclusion. But I guess they gave me rotten advice. No wonder their company is going into Chapter 11. Hope you can see your way clear to overlook this *faux pas*."

Skulking around the office, oozing into corners and closets to avoid facing the consequences of a disastrous mistake made by your nearest and dearest, may, in fact, earn you exoneration this time. If you can just manage to hang onto your job.

Unfortunately, your spouse, children and friends will be waiting anxiously to find out how their "help" helped. You should answer with a sad smile:

> You: "Yeah. It nearly got me canned! Fine wife (or husband or son or daughter) you turned out to be! How could you have misled me this way?"

But then, to make them feel a little bit better, just add:

> You: Oh, it's not all your fault, though. It's mine. I should have known that you couldn't possibly know enough to make the right call on something as complicated as this.

Friends and family give the person trying not to make a mistake at least three important advantages:

1. It gives you at least some basis for deciding something you know too little about. And which decision will be judged to be wrong in any event.

2. It gives you someone to blame when things shrink and shrivel — someone your superiors can more easily forgive than you. Why fire old Joe just because he has a stupid wife?

3. It teaches youngsters the perils of decision-making. They will soon learn that, since they can never manage to make a correct decision, it is better for them to make none. It will teach them Dodge #9, a lesson they'll thank you for later in life. Too bad you didn't learn it when you were their age. You wouldn't be in such bad shape if you had!

You might think it unconscionable that we would advocate using your husband, wife, child, poker club associates and Yoga classmates to provide cover for your own indiscreet business misdeeds. But look, this is your career you are trying to save. And, these days, your career has a fifty-fifty chance of lasting longer than your marriage.

Chapter Nine

Special Rules for Men vs. Women

Sex Issues in Arriving at Decisions

Now, with men and women increasingly sharing front-office responsibilities in the corporate world, there are a growing number of issues that revolve about something we call gender-based decision evasion. It's a whole new science of business-place sexual interaction and deserves a chapter of its own. This is it.

With the growing importance of women in corporate life, the shattering of the glass ceiling, and the possibility that your boss may as easily be a woman as a man, you must learn to use the opposite sex as an agent in your exploitation of Dodge #9.

The Female Decision-Evader

Let's talk about businesswomen first. There are, happily, ever more of them breaking their way into positions of corporate responsibility. These women need to know how to use the men around them when they want to employ Dodge #9 to evade responsibility for making a decision. Of course, they can use all of the material presented thus far in order to achieve success in commerce and industry. They will also, naturally, be able to use the material in this chapter to escape the consequences of having inadvertently made a decision.

73

Which brings up the matter of the feminist movement. Now this may upset the hell out of Steinem, Friedan, Ireland, and the more dedicated of their followers, but it's the truth: A woman, by simply being a woman, has a great many additional weapons at her command to help her escape the need to ever make a decision. The use of these supplemental tactics of responsibility-evasion is a matter of instinct for a normal woman; she uses them reflexively, without conscious effort. They just happen. But remember, the time will never come when you will not be conscious of the fact that you are a woman and he isn't. However, in the interest of presenting a text that is comprehensive and complete in every detail, the following female-only options are listed.

When faced with a decision-situation, a woman can...

1. Hide behind her own skirts. No matter what her position of authority in the organization, a woman can always step back into the role of female consultant and disassociate herself from the business at hand.

> She: "I'm just here to give you the female slant on things, not to give you guys all the answers. You'll have to decide what to do about it by yourself."

In this way, women can still manage to give the impression that, when all is said and done, they are still relative newcomers in the world of business, still standing a bit on the sidelines. Not a bad place to be. Even though they control 51% of the dollars on Wall Street.

2. Adopt the "It's a man's world" defense. This is a subtle variation on the tactic of hiding behind her own skirts and is based on the assumption still held by many macho types that a woman isn't really smart enough to cut the mustard in the world of dog-eat-dog business. An obvious misconception, but one that a woman can

still exploit in certain circumstances. The script goes like this:

> You: "I have never really understood what you
> men are doing. So please just ignore me as I
> stand here on the sidelines and try to learn
> from you. I have no opinion on this, and you
> really can't expect me, a mere woman in a
> man's world, to have one, now can you?"

3. She can be the girl next door and go all soft and feminine—no matter how steely and self-assured she is in her heart. This has to do with hormones and traditional masculine-feminine roles. A slight hint of a Southern accent sometimes helps.

> You: "Now you just pay no mind to li'l ole me. I
> just so admire the way you big guys can size
> up a situation and do something about it,
> while we girls just flutter around so and
> never make up our minds about anything."

This kind of line can drive even the most masculine of men into the most ill-considered and intemperate decisions. You've got to be something of an ass in this day and age to fall for it. But it's sometimes worth a shot.

4. Be "ill." A woman has times of functional illness— menstrual cycles, yeast infections, light bladder control problems (and all the other plumbing failures that most men learn about from television commercials)—during which she simply cannot be forced into doing anything she doesn't want to do. Like making a decision.

Since it would be indelicate for her associates to watch the calendar and thereby keep tabs on her "difficult" days (and what could they do about it, even if they did?), a woman can pretend to be having menstrual cramps and/or P.M.S. as often as once every thirteen days and get away with it. Thirteen days is about as long as most men can remember anything about a woman, including her birthday. In addition, women are subject to emotional storms for other reasons—ranging from menopause to their inability to get a beauty salon appointment at a convenient time—none of which any man can possibly understand. But all of which can become legitimate reasons for avoiding business decisions. A woman can be ill on cue as often as required and never have the same illness twice.

5. If you were brought up in the seventies, you can become suddenly militant. Interpret the situation as an attack on all women and shout, "Male chauvinist pig!" at every man in the room. Then shove your chest forward and snarl something like, "And I refuse to wear a bra just to protect you from your exploitive masculine sexist fantasies!" This is an old female business-place ploy that dates back to the 1960s, but one which most men have still not yet defensed against. As a result, after such a feminist outburst, no man will ever have gumption enough to pursue the matter at hand any further. He will usually take the initiative and make the decision himself instead of risking another outburst.

6. Cry. A woman in tears is a natural event, like rain on a cloudy day or robins flying south for the winter. Yet it upsets men and can even upset other women (but less often). Everyone concerned usually wants to make the waterfalls stop as soon as possible, and is willing to do almost anything to accomplish this end. Therefore, a woman may effectively cry either to avoid making a decision in the first place, or to avoid suffering the consequences after having made one. No woman in tears can ever be held responsible for anything, and that fact has largely followed women into the workplace. A man

will get fired for a bad decision. A woman who can cry movingly just gets sympathy.

7. A woman can be immoral. It's the oldest dodge of all, and still the best. Sleeping around is a sin that can cover a multitude of sins.

So much for the ways in which a woman can avoid the pitfalls of corporate decision-making. The problem now is, how can men avoid having women force them into making decisions? It's hard to do. Fortunately, however, it is still, mostly, a man's world (see #3 above) and the one decision every man will forgive another for making is the decision a woman talked him into. Which brings us to...

How Men Can Handle Women Decision-Evaders

In the last couple of decades, the sexuality of the workplace has changed, and before a man can learn to hand off decision-responsibility to a woman, he has to understand a few things about how the rules have changed. Thanks to Betty, NOW and Gloria, there has been an explosion of women's rights in the workplace. What our fathers referred to patronizingly as "Women's Lib" and its bra-less militancy has become something called "feminism" and you had better look out! The Nine Old Men of the Supreme Court now include Two Old Ladies. Women own more of America than ever before. And there are more ladies in corner offices these days than there are in the secretarial pool.

Then there is sexual harassment. It has reared its aggressive head against men in the workplace, in the military, in Congressional hearings about Supreme Court nominees and even in presidential impeachment trials. These days, women have an easier time dealing with men in the workplace than men have dealing with women. Women are seldom seen as sexual aggressors in the business world, no matter how aggressive they are in business situations. But men are always seen as potential sexist Neanderthals.

A sin that covers a multitude of sins

Men have had to learn to use gender-neutral language, have had to learn to pretend not to notice that women are women, have had to forget about holding doors, letting women go first, remembering anniversaries. They have had to learn not to touch women where women can touch men, have learned not to leer when they smile, not to stare (or even look) at breasts, legs and rear ends, not to tell off-color jokes and to avoid double entendres. What a man may consider just a friendly wink can become an unwelcome advance to juries deciding sexual harassment cases.

It may, in fact, take several more generations before all of the implications of the sexual revolution are digested into our business culture. But there are many things a man can do to entice women co-workers, female corporate colleagues and even his women bosses, to accept decision-responsibility when he doesn't want to. He can appeal to her female nurturing instincts, her sense of intuition, her intelligence and her business acumen. He can use flattery, sweet talk and a subservient attitude (just as many men do in handling their marriage partners) and win the non-decision with one of those manly wiles.

But always keep this in mind: You will never get to the place where you won't be acutely aware of the fact that she's female and you're not.

Here are a few pointers every man should observe when dealing with a woman co-worker or a female superior:

1. Never flex a muscle in her presence.

2. When sharing meals, never have a drink unless she does and then pretend that you always order white wine.

3. No Playboy magazines visible in your office, and no automotive supply company calendars on your walls, please.

4. When with her alone, in your office or hers, be sure to talk about your wife, your girlfriend or significant other — even if you have to make it all up. That way she will not feel that she is a sex object in your eyes.

It is becoming harder and harder to pin decision-responsibility on a woman. As we have indicated, a man should never try to get a woman to make a decision in ways that men usually seek to get women to do what they want them to do. Never praise their beauty, their nifty figures, their flowing hair, limpid eyes, luscious lips. That doesn't work in a working-together culture. Instead, appeal to those assets that all women think they have over men.

Here are a few ways you may be able to do it:

1. Appeal to her nurturing instincts. It is probably related to hormones, but most women fall into a nurturing mode naturally in the proper circumstances. They want to take care of the weak and protect the neediest around them. They do it with children, with old folks, with the homeless. If you can appeal to the mother in the woman you are trying to con into relieving you of the responsibility for making a decision, whether she is your peer, your superior or your junior, you can easily get her to make the decisions you don't want to make. Sample discussion:

> You: "Gee, I really don't know which way to go
> on this. What do you suggest?"

Look at her with a childlike plea in your eye, quiver your lip a little if you can manage it. If your name is John or James, try thinking of yourself as Johnny or Jimmy. Sort of like Method Acting.

> She: "Well, just you don't worry a bit about that.
> I'll do it for you."

Aha! The deed has been done. You feel protected and she feels protective. What could be nicer than that?

2. Appeal to her intuition. Intuition is that innate sense that all women just know they have. So try to make her intuition work for you. Like this:

> You: "Mary (or Ms. Parker, if she's your boss), you always seem to have such an unerring intuition about things like this. But I never seem to get it right. What does that inner you think about this? I really need to know."

> She: "Well, since you ask, this is what I feel about this...."

Whatever she says, that's the decision. Made by her — not by you. Whatever happens, you are completely safe.

3. Women are, by nature, teachers. They love to educate. Which is why you find more women than men teaching kindergarten and first grade. You may be able to convince a woman you work with to make a decision by appealing to that innate desire to educate. Like this:

> You: "I wish you'd show me how to do this. I never seem to know what I should do first. Teach me, will you please?"

> She: "Okay, stand back and watch how I manage to get it done."

See? She can't resist. It's the urge to educate. Good. She's made the necessary decision.

4. Flattery will get you everywhere with a woman. But, in a corporate environment, you can't flatter a woman by telling her how beautiful she is, how you like her new dress or the way she's now doing her hair. That would be overtly sexist. Instead, you must flatter her

intellect, her brain, her smarts. Since most women think they are just naturally smarter than men (it's a hormonal girl thing), you can win a woman into making a decision by appealing to her hormonal sense of superiority. For example:

> You: "Boy, you're so smart about this kind of
> stuff. You remind me of my dad (but never
> your mom!), he always knew the right
> answer in cases like this! So, what do you
> think we should do?" (Note the "we."
> Women always like to do things in a part-
> nering sort of way.)

> She: "Well, I do have an opinion (all women
> always have an opinion!) about that. I think
> we should do thus and so...."

So take her advice. Voilà! The decision is made.

5. Marry her. Sometimes it's worth it. Then you are only half responsible for any consequences.

Today, when dealing with women in decision-situations, men should remember that chivalry is dead and that Maid Marion is now a tough old bitch ready to knee you in the groin if you cross her. We've tried to show you how to break through the defenses she has put in your way. Yes, you can get the women in your company to relieve you of decision responsibility. But be careful!

As we have demonstrated, men and women in the corporate world both have an investment in avoiding decisions whose consequences will interfere with achieving CEO status. Once upon a time, women didn't have so much to worry about since so few of them were ever able to graduate out of the secretarial pool, penetrate the glass ceiling and reach a position where a decision was ever required. But things have changed mightily, haven't they?

Part II

How to Escape a Bad Decision After You've Made It

Chapter Ten

How Not to Pay the Piper

Turning Failure into Success

To this point, we have discussed the vital importance of avoiding responsibility by avoiding decisions. As we have demonstrated, there is no better way to achieve success in the world of business, government, education, the military — you name it. We have carefully demonstrated a comprehensive repertoire of tried and true techniques by which this avoidance can be accomplished, even by novices. The Harvard School of Business cannot teach you more on this important subject — and would probably teach you less if given the opportunity.

Nevertheless, it must be conceded that most ordinary men or women are simply not capable of *not* making decisions without a great deal of experience in the evasive arts. There is bound to be backsliding, especially among middle and lower rank executives who are neither as experienced nor as wise as those who have, through careful decision-evasion, achieved higher status.

For this reason, we have chosen to devote the second section of this book to a recitation of proven methods by which those who inadvertently commit a decision during the course of a career can escape the consequences thereof.

It should be pointed out, however, that these are extreme measures and should be invoked no more than half a dozen times during the course of an ordinary business career. If you feel yourself compelled to make decisions too frequently, this is a sign that you are unsuited to business life. You should, in this event, attempt to carve out a career in a field less hazardous. The postal service and sanitation suggest themselves as arenas in which the opportunity to make a decision seldom, if ever, arises. You would find them completely safe.

Here, then, is a comprehensive compendium of ways in which to evade responsibility for decisions that you somehow accidentally make during periods of weakness of will.

To set the stage, let's imagine the lid has just blown off a decision you are responsible for having made. The rumble has shaken the company to its foundations, and you hear that top management is even now drafting a letter asking for your resignation. What should you do?

1. The first thing to do is to fire someone on your staff— quick. Or fire several people. Have a stable of heads ready to roll at all times. It is absolutely necessary to swing your sword in a very wide arc; the punishment should always far more than fit the crime. The more violent your reaction, no matter how inconsequential the decision you got caught making, the less likely it is that anyone will pin the responsibility on you. Your superiors will naturally assume that the people whom you have dismissed were guilty of conniving in the decision without your knowledge. And the worst you may then expect is a mild reprimand for having hired such disloyal, incompetent and untrustworthy people. You're safe!

2. Admit the fact of the decision, but find someone else to blame. You have a wide array of candidates to select from. The information you got from the research department was dead wrong; anyone given the facts you were handed would have decided the matter

Find someone else to blame

exactly as you did. There was no choice. Or the advice you received from the people in the field, the people in sales and marketing, the people at the factory, the people on your own staff, was way off the mark in every important respect. Or your secretary garbled a key message or acted most unwisely in your absence. Or a combination of all of these factors.

All of these are defenses that people aware of Dodge #9 would mount to get out of from under a load of blame. But they don't always work. What you do, however, after finding lots of people and things to blame for the wrongo decision, is to...

3. Accept all the blame yourself! Demand to have it! Naturally, no one will let you have the blame since, by accepting blame, you have just proven what a sweet person you are. Just as you can't give away credit (as we will explain in a moment), so you cannot be given blame, even when you pretend that you want to. It just won't rub off. Mea culpa is a great defense if you are talented enough to make people think that you actually mean it.

4. Be a bemoaner. Pretend that the decision you are charged with making came from elsewhere and that you were not its originator, but simply its unwilling vehicle. Give the impression that you were overruled and forced to act as you did. Bemoan the whole episode by saying such things as, "If they had only listened to me!" or, "I tried to tell them what would happen, but you know how *they* are, once they've made up their minds."

Don't identify "they." But try to give the impression that "they" are higher-ups in the organization.

This is an excellent ploy to use among your peers who might otherwise tend to gloat over your bad fortune. By

implying that you were the carrier of a decision formu-
lated by more senior members of the company, you let
your equals know that you are more equal than they
are and held in higher regard by the important people
you both work for. Always finish by saying something
like, "Well, thank God it's not *my* fault."

Sometimes, of course, you must do your bemoaning to
higher ups, in which case your position should be that
your peers are the idiots to blame and that, surrounded
as you are by incompetents, it is amazing that you are
able to manage as well as you do. Then use the above
"thank God" line and hope for the best.

5. Distract attention from your failure by suddenly creating a great deal of furor about the real or imagined
failures of others in the organization. No one can put on
a more convincing holier-than-thou act than the unholi-
est of all. Write memoranda that begin, "It has come to
my attention that the New Products Department was
caught out on a limb again last week by the Ipso Factory people. This sort of thing cannot be allowed to con-
tinue. Following are my proposals for insuring against
future failures of this nature...." And so on.

Send copies to as many people as you can think of. Top
management always appreciates people who can take
the broad view. And they may be convinced to over-
look your most recent transgression. But you can't do
this more than half a dozen times.

6. Turn your obvious failure into an obvious success
through the sheer strength of your conviction. This is
the hardest route to absolution, but very effective if you
can manage to make it convincing. So few people have
deep convictions about anything these days that they
are often deeply impressed by someone who does.

A strong and impassioned display of conviction is almost embarrassing to them, like seeing a grown man cry. Therefore, maintain hotly that the so-called failure was actually a magnificent success—and that the results accomplished were exactly the results you sought. Pretend indignation (righteous) and amazement (incredulous) when others fail to see the fine points involved as clearly as you do.

If you are forceful and insistent enough, you may actually be able to win a good many supporters for your position. Keep at it and your adversaries will soon begin to doubt their own views and suspect that, perhaps, you see things more clearly than they do. You may even be able to work the episode into a promotion; management is often impressed by what it doesn't understand.

However, if the decision was a real bomb, you may not be able to get away with this technique.

7. Eventually, if the weight of opinion remains adamantly against you, concede nobly and say, with a philosophic shrug of your shoulders, "Well, if I had only known that you wanted to *keep* the Smithers account instead of losing it, why, that would have been easy!" Thus the mistake becomes nothing more serious than a misunderstanding.

Be warned that these tactics are to be used only as a last resort, and sparingly. If used too frequently, they lose their effectiveness. You are far better off, of course, if you can avoid using them. There are, after all, only five of these escape routes. If you're not frugal with them, they will be all gone before you get promoted out of the mailroom.

Chapter Eleven

Some Decisions You *Can* Make

Booboos, Bobbles and Boners

No man or woman wants to be a complete cipher in life. Everyone needs to make some kind of decision from time to time. It's human nature. It's the only way we have to prove our worth to those whose good opinion we want to have. We need to be able to impress our kids, hold our own with supermarket cashiers and have our neighbors' high regard, even when they drive nicer cars and have lusher lawns than we do. So an occasional decision isn't all bad.

While the purpose of this book is to help you to NEVER make a decision, we also know that if you can't rear up and bellow "This is what I WANT!" from time to time, life will be dull as death. As indicated earlier, the need to have opinions and make decisions is hard-wired into our psyches from infancy. It's something we must do to lead full lives.

But, if you want to live a successful life, you must pick your decision arenas with care. What you are looking for are decisions to make that will demonstrate your intellectual leadership without bothering anybody. You must find decisions to make that make no difference, decisions that have no consequences, decisions you can laugh off if they turn out disastrously. Such decisions must be of the kind that will not directly affect your business life. They must impact other people only peripherally.* Their outcomes must not be important to anyone except, perhaps, you. And finally, the decisions you make must not cost any money. Within these parameters, you are free to fulfill all of your dreams of being a leader of men and/or women.

However, even under these circumstances, if the decisions you make turn out badly, you still need a way to escape being blamed for them. Fortunately, there is a whole category of bonehead decisions that everyone is willing to laugh off without condemning the decision maker to a life of low-level achievement. We call them "Booboos, Bobbles and Boners." Used skillfully, they can turn even the most egregious decision into a laughing matter. When people are laughing at you, they can't be mad at you. It's a rule of life. That's why there are court jesters and Bill Cosby.

> 1. *Booboos* are one class of judgement that can simply be shrugged off if things go south. "Boy, was that a dumb thing to do," you admit with a light laugh. "I don't know what I was thinking! By now you should know me well enough to see that I can't ever be trusted to do the right thing in circumstances like these. Ha-ha! After this, just don't listen to me anymore, okay?" Laugh again and see if you can get the other person to laugh back. A laugh back is equal to forgiveness.

> There are office booboos — like using the wrong Internet search engine or sending the Smith order to the Jones Company. There are family booboos, like driving your family to the beach this summer when all (except you) unanimously decided to go to the mountains. Or taking your spouse out to a new ethnic restaurant and discovering that the chef was trained at Leavenworth.

---

* Like where you park your car, which building entrance you use, where you order-in lunch from.

"Sorry," you explain. "I just thought this would be better. I'm such a dummy. Everyone, please forgive me."

There are relationship booboos, like calling your wife by your girlfriend's name (or vice versa) or forgetting your anniversary or a kid's birthday. The less time you spend at home, the less time your significant other has to ream you out. Nasty, but not fatal. See you down at Clancy's. Or at the beauty shop.

There are man-to-man and woman-to-woman booboos, like touting the Bears or the Cubs against the Packers or the Braves, or recommending a beauty shop that turns out to give lousy perms. When your best friend comes back with a hairdo that would frighten Godzilla, you ease out of the blame game by saying, "Boy! What a booboo!" You shrug and try to look cute. And don't forget—laugh.

No one will ever let a plain and simple booboo come between you and a successful career. Though there are some booboos that may screw up your home life forever.

2. *Boners* are mistakes you make because you haven't been paying attention. You read the script wrong and the words come out backwards. Or you fail to add the totals on the second page to the totals on the first page to get a bottom-line total on a spreadsheet. Bookkeepers do it all the time, even with calculators and Quicken. Another boner is ordering lunch for fifteen when you have seventeen mouths to feed. Or failing to *cc* your boss on an important memo not addressed to him or her. Or taking the kids to the soccer field when they should have gone to ballet class. Happens to all of us.

"What a bonehead thing for me to do," you laugh. "I'll never live this down, I guess." This dialog is designed to get the recipient of your boner to say something like, "Forget it. It was an honest mistake."

3. *Bobbles* are failures to follow through, failures to achieve a clean pass in the relay race of business. You were supposed to tell Mr. CEO Sweeney what John Research discovered about the failure of the company's new product to lock onto the market. But you forgot. Or you were supposed to pick up the cleaning before you drove home last evening. But you forgot. Or your husband left an important note for you on the refrigerator door about expecting company tonight, but you forgot to check the refrigerator door. A bobble is like a basketball player not being able to get a handle on the ball and letting it roll out of bounds.

Not good, any of these bobbles. But not fatal, if you handle the situation properly:

> "I'm sorry," you say (still smiling), "I really
> dropped the ball on that one, didn't I? Well,
> not to worry. It won't happen again, I prom-
> ise."

Of course, it probably will happen again — but by then you hope that the bobblee will have forgotten who it was who pulled off the first bobble.

Booboos, boners and bobbles won't kill you, if you can just learn to laugh them off, and get others to laugh with you. They are foolproof escape mechanisms that allow you to actually decide something from time to time without striking out on your whole career. It will do a world of good to your self-esteem to have actually decided something — especially if you can escape the consequences by claiming a booboo, a bobble or a boner.

Remember, it is not bad decisions that will pillory you, but bad decisions about things that people really care about.

Never Try to Be TOO Successful!

Even executives who are already expert at the application of Dodge #9 in their business lives sometimes forget the rules when they have managed to climb part of the way up the ladder.

This often happens to bright men and women. Dodge Niners who, having gotten their successes broadcast in the industry (Trade papers are great, aren't they?), are hired away from the firms where they have achieved their reputations to "save" another company from disaster.

It happened to Sidney S. who was wooed away from one Madison ad agency to save another by improving its new business activities and winning new clients. The money was good, the office was larger, and the hierarchy thinner, so his chance to become the lead player looked pretty good.

But Sidney S. forgot the Guidelines of Dodge #9 that had boosted his career so far and vaingloriously actually set about to sharpen his new company's client solicitation procedures. He was successful at it. Single-handedly Sid managed to bring several millions of dollars in new billing into the agency. Trade papers celebrated his success. Even The Wall Street Journal took notice. An industry "underground" newsletter reported that he would soon "take over" the agency. He got a substantial raise. Things looked good.

Then one day he was fired. Just like that. And, too late, he realized that he had forgotten all about Dodge #9. The last thing the president and two executive VPs of the new agency wanted was someone who would be successful on his own, and therefore threaten their authority. What they were really looking for was a guy who would sit around the office and schmooze with them while they casually discussed strategies and decided nothing. All they wanted was Sidney's reputation, not any ability he might have. If Sid had just talked with the other executives and not tried to actually decide something, he'd still be at the agency. The agency failed two years after Sid's departure.

Chapter Twelve

The Last Resort

When All Else Fails...

In spite of your best efforts, there will still be times when a decision seeks you out to be made no matter what evasive actions you have taken. Whatever you do, don't panic. For, no matter how bad the situation looks, there are still ways to escape the consequences of decision-making—if you are diligent. So pay attention.

The first step you will have to take may seem somewhat paradoxical: You must actually learn how to make decisions! But these must be carefully qualified decisions that still leave the monkey of responsibility on someone else's back. In extreme cases, you must be willing to forget the natural sense of fair play that is so basic a part of your sterling character, and pin the rap on one of your own subordinates. After all, what are subordinates for? This is no time to be a Boy Scout.

Imagine, now, that a decision-situation has broken through all of your early-warning systems and reached your desk. Here are seven ways to deal with it:

1. Buck the decision up, down, or sideways.

    a. *Upward bucking:* If your immediate supervisor is smart, he may not allow you to buck the decision up to him, even if your request that he "review" the situation is couched in a properly plaintive and subservient memo composed to massage his ego:

> You: "I really need your help on this, sir (or madam). No one understands matters of this nature better than you do, sir (or madam). We'd be very grateful if you would give us a hand with it."

b. *Sideways bucking:* Sideways bucking requires a certain sense of peremptory authority in the operative memo you write to the head of a parallel department in the company:

> "Jeanne, this is a matter for your decision. Please handle and advise. T. M. Wortling."

Notice that the "and advise" phrase in this memo not only sticks Jeanne (or John or Madge) with the decision, but leaves you one up on her (or him) as well.

c. *Downward bucking:* Downward bucking must be done with an air of irritable exasperation to be effective: Your memo should say something like:

> "John, I wish your people would learn to handle matters like the enclosed more efficiently. I am much too busy to take the time, considering my heavy workload, to do this for you every time it comes up. Such matters *must* be handled before they reach my desk. T.M.W."

2. Call a meeting of your people, give them the problem and, pleading business elsewhere, tell them to solve it. Your exit line is:

> "Do whatever you like, people. I'll back you on
> it."

Of course, you'll back them only if the decision they make actually works.

However, if through some strange accident they *are* successful, you must give them full credit, much as this may go against the grain. There are two reasons for this: First, because you may need to have them repeat the process next week and, second, because you will thus enhance your own image. As we have pointed out earlier, you really *can't* give away credit, try as you may. The more you tell others what a great job your gang did, the more they will be convinced that it was your great leadership that helped them carry the day.

If your people are too smart to go it alone and insist that you review a decision they have made before putting it into action, your line is:

> You: "Well, that's not exactly the way I would
> have done it, but go ahead anyway."

Criticize no further, as if loath to nitpick a decision you have been too busy to help formulate. If it then turns out to have been an improper decision, for whatever reason, you are free to say something like,

> "It's funny, but the thing old J. B. objected to is
> exactly the thing I was afraid of — but I
> didn't want to say anything at the time."

They'll love you for your tolerant attitude.

3. Be decisively vague in passing a problem down. Give your people directions that, while forceful, are also unclear, self-conflicting and subject to many interpretations. Tell them exactly what to do, but not exactly. A good preface in such a situation is:

> You: "Now, this shouldn't be too tough. All we
> have to do, as I see it, is..." and then ramble
> on incoherently about things in general. Fin-
> ish up with: "This all needs development, of
> course, but I'll leave that all up to you capa-
> ble people."

All will nod eagerly and not discover that you have
given them no useful direction until they are back in
their windowless cubbyholes.

4. If you can't get away with decisive vagaries, give
more explicit but *divergent* directions to two or more
subordinate groups. This always gives you an out since
you can later go along with the more successful solution and claim that the others were the result of misun-
derstandings:

> You: "I don't see how the Jones group could
> have gotten so far off base."

5. Another rather tricky but often successful way of
evading decision-responsibility is the "consistent
answer" method. This consists simply of *always* saying
yes or *always* saying no, no matter what the question or
the circumstances, and no matter what others may be
urging you to say.

If you decide to be a "no-sayer," you must expect to be
disobeyed, since things *must* get done in spite of what
you say. They will be done behind your back, so you
cannot be considered responsible for them. "No-sayers"
get a great reputation for decisiveness, but they tend to
be disliked. You may not be able to stand the pressure if
you like to be loved.

It is therefore somewhat easier to become a "yes-
sayer" — to say yes blandly, blindly and with a pleasant
smile to all people and all questions. Your associates

will soon understand that your yes means nothing more than "it's all up to you," and they will be responsible in any case. But they will always defend you because you are so damned likable.

Yes-saying is better than no-saying for several additional reasons. If you are a "yes-sayer," you are not only better liked by your associates, but each will feel that he has your ear and your confidence. A meeting with you never produces tension. This improves overall morale in your department. And since you will say yes to even the most opposing of propositions, the final yes or no will have to come from somewhere else eventually. Wherever it comes from, it isn't your fault.

6. Keep any decision you are forced to make a secret until all the results are in. This is a difficult trick to manage, but it can be done on occasion. If the results of a decision appear to be negative, you are free to remake the decision the other way around, and no one will be the wiser. This sort of ballet dancing requires that you work all alone, or with a few mild-mannered, browbeaten underlings.

7. The last retreat, the last resort, the last defense against decision-making is to qualify. When absolutely cornered by a decision that is screaming to be made, temporize. Make a forthright decision hedged by protective provisos. Here are a few tested versions of well qualified decisions:

You: "If the decision to be made is as you
    describe it, Joe, my answer is yes."

or

You: "If your research is what you say it is,
    Susan, my answer is no."

You have thus made the required decision but left yourself a barndoor-sized loophole if punitive responsibility must later be pinned on someone.

Another limited decision technique:

> You: "For the time being, yes."

or

> "Temporarily no. But check with me later."

The imaginary suggestion technique:

> You: "I'll go along—this once—with your suggestion, Tom."

This is effective whether Tom has actually made a suggestion or not. He will be flattered to think that you think he did!

One of the most effective ways to qualify a decision is to ask other people what they think the boss wants.

> You: "Well, what does Quigley think—what does he want to do?" (Quigley, of course, is the corporate head honcho.)

There is sure to be at least one person in the company who fancies himself an expert at second-guessing the CEO. He'll tell you what Quigley wants done. So do it. You're in the clear. The second-guesser is the decision-maker who will take the heat when the time comes.

> You: "But I thought you really knew."

As should be obvious from all that has gone before, a prudent business executive need never get stuck behind the eight ball of a decision; need never accept responsibility for anything he or she does or doesn't do. Naturally, it's not an easy thing to manage. Many treacherous pitfalls line the road up the mountain of success. That is why so few actually ever make it to the top.

But now, with this little manual, even you have a chance to make it. Use your intelligence. Be a wary observer in every situation and keep your wits about you. And you may avoid ever being blamed for anything. You may avoid ever being forced to make a decision. You may therefore *never make a mistake*.

Dodge #9 will see you through. All the way.

REALITY SNAPSHOT:
Say YES and Be a Winner

Bill S., one of the most successful Madison Avenue executives of all time, was an accomplished "yes-sayer." He was the fourth man on the totem pole (for good reason) when his ad agency was founded. But, in the fullness of time, Bill bubbled to the top and ran his advertising agency by adhering faithfully to the tenets of Dodge #9—never making a decision. His way of doing it was to always say yes whenever he was asked to decide something. The last man or woman out of Bill's office always carried the day. His company, immobilized by his cautious indecision, finally teetered on the brink of failure.

But the yes-saying executive's reputation for never making a wrong move had become well known in his industry. Other large advertising companies were eager to have such an infallible genius on their team. So the "yes-sayer" finally said his last yes—to an attractive merger proposition—and made a fortune. His new associates soon discovered why he was so infallible and retired him as soon as they could. He didn't give a damn. He was rich.

Chapter Thirteen[*]

The Soft Landing Strategy

Finding a Way Out When You Really Want to Stay In

Getting fired because they ended up on the downside of a decision is the worst nightmare of those of who have been snookered into saying yes or no when they should have said nothing. You'd think they'd have learned!

But even if you are one of these poor souls, there are a few ploys that can snatch life from the jaws of death, that can get a bad situation reversed and a pink slip rescinded. But it takes a bit of brass to pull them off. You've always got to be prepared to have your bluff called. If you don't really have the career straight flush you've been bragging about, it's off to the unemployment office for you.

We list these ploys here for your consideration:

1. The "Go ahead, fire me!" defense. Act like you don't really give a damn. Suggest slyly during the separation interview that there are several other companies bidding for your body, but that you have, out of corporate loyalty, spurned their rich offers.

---

[*] Thirteen. An unfortunate number for any business text. We had thought of skipping it entirely, as some buildings skip a thirteenth floor. But since this book is about reality, we have chosen to use it.

If you do this with enough self-confident aplomb, you may be able to convince your superior that, if you are worth more to a competitor than you are being paid in your old job here, there must be something worthwhile about you after all. Though they haven't been able to find out what it is yet.

In which case, you may be asked to stay—and accept a salary a few percent ahead of what you suggested another company was willing to pay. Not too shabby a result after having cost your company a bundle through sheer wrong-headedness.

2. The good good-bye. A second and related gambit is to say, with a deep sigh, "Well, okay, I guess it's best for me to leave. You know, I've gotten a little bored with the way things are going around here. My father-in-law is in the gold mine business and he has been begging me to join the company. I guess I should, right?"

This approach will shock the person in charge of giving you your walking papers. The truth is that it is no fun to fire a person who doesn't give a damn if you fire him/her or not. Since there will be no begging, no groveling, no mea culpa for the person doing the firing to enjoy, he might as well just keep you on staff. What the hell.

3. A third strategy is to talk up your value to the company. "Go ahead, get rid of me! Like who is going to do a better job than I did? Nobody, that's who!" That's right: guts it out. Get red in the face. Wave your arms. Stand up and pace the floor.

Your company may decide, at the last minute, to keep you on the roster just because they like to have a passionate scapegoat around to sop up the pools of blame that occasionally slosh through the offices. It takes experience to become a perfect scapegoat, the one who is always there to take the blame for everything bad that happens; the bad coffee maker, the broken copy machine, the fouled up intranet server. The executive you report to may decide to stick with the scapegoat he has than go off into uncharted waters trying to train a new one.

4. Or you can pretend relief at the turn of events. "Well, I guess this comes at a good time for me. I've been thinking of getting into the business for myself, anyhow. So now I can do it. Great!"

The implied threat that you will soon be in competition with your company, after studying the business at their expense all these years, and learning all of their secrets from the inside, will tend to raise second thoughts on their part. Maybe, they'll figure, it's better to suffer the fools we have than to try to find new ones to suffer.

5. Find a safety net. Stay on the job market at all times, even when things at the office are going great. Keep your résumé up to date and properly inflated. Call a headhunter now and then just to check in. Keep your network with old college chums and colleagues plugged in, chatting with them as often as you can.

The idea is to build a roster of soft landings so you always have someplace to go when push comes to shove. The easier it is to find a new job, the easier it will be to tell your old boss to shove it.

6. The Family Plan. If you think there is no way for you to keep your old job, start talking it up to your in-laws and your Uncle Mort (the one who owns all the auto dealerships). Tell them how great you are doing at your company, how much your superiors love you, and all about the fast track you're on towards that big corner office. After a few years of this treatment, some of your

relatives-in-law may begin to think that the loser who married their Dick or Jane isn't quite as stupid as everyone thought. Maybe they'll find a job for him in the family business after all.

The softest landing after getting kicked out of a job, is to have a job in the family business. You've *really* got to screw up in order to get fired from that job. And when you tell the boss who is firing you of your good fortune, he'll envy you. He may even keep you on the job just so that you don't enjoy life more than he does!

7. Transfer out. Finally, when you are nailed for repeatedly screwing up your job in one department of your company, you may put off the final bye-bye pink slip by asking for a transfer to another department.

For example, you may suggest that you could do much better in the marketing department than you have done in the engineering department. "Working over there," you assure your boss, "is much more suited to my training." Look sincere.

There are several advantages to using this gambit. If you can manage to get yourself transferred rather than dismissed, your salary may not be reduced. Your retirement and medical benefits may be unaffected and you'll not have to change your commuting routine. Besides, your boss (who really gets sick to his stomach whenever he has to fire someone) will love the opening you have given him to escape his guilt.

Once you are in the new department, with new superiors, new colleagues, new offices, you'll have a clean slate. You can start making bad decisions all over again. It may take years for them to catch up with you this time. You might even suggest to some of those new colleagues that you are a transfer, sent over temporarily just to straighten out the mess in their department. That'll earn you some respect.

The more departments in your company, the more often you can pull this trick. In a really multi-national outfit, you can repeat it until retirement.

The point we are urging on you in this chapter is not to go gently into that dark night. Sneak your way back onto the company roster any way you can. Never accept a pink slip with bowed head and hangdog expression. Pretend that you never expected it, that it is certainly unjust, and that you don't really give a damn. Their loss is your gain. You'll do better wherever you land. Make them think that there are lots of organizations out there who are hot for your body. That may make them hotter for your body than they have been to date.

Tell them angrily that you have been a great asset to the company, whether management is smart enough to see that or not! Still, because your uncle may not hire you after all, and the organizations bidding for your services may not actually make you an offer, what you'd like most is forgiveness. When you've stymied yourself by making bad decisions and suffered the mistakes that flow from them, the thing you need most is forgiveness.

Epilogue

Nothing Ventured, Nothing Blamed

This text is finished. Now you know the golden secret, the *real* secret of achieving success in business: now you know what Dodge #9 is all about.

NEVER MAKE A DECISION
AND YOU'LL NEVER MAKE A MISTAKE

And you have also learned dozens of ways to escape decision-making and its consequences. The author has tried to demonstrate the high hazards of rushing headlong into the resolution of problems, and to distill into the fewest possible words the rules of the game of responsibility-denial, which have been developed and are used by many of today's most successful leaders.

The author has also tried to arm you against your own misguided enthusiasms by showing you how to cover your tracks when a decision bubbles forth involuntarily and you must avoid the consequences you so richly deserve.

But reading and understanding these rules is only the first step. You must commit them to memory so that they remain forever burned into the forefront of your mind. You must make them part of your innermost instinct for survival in a world that is *always* looking for someone to blame. The best way to do this is to practice faithfully. You may find it helpful, for example, to put these rules to use in your home life as well as in your business life — by refusing to make decisions about where to have dinner when you go out, whether to go to the shore or to the mountains on vacation, whom to invite to cocktail parties, how to punish the children when they misbehave, which TV channel to watch on Monday nights. In this way, Dodge #9, the art of responsibility evasion, will become second nature to you.

Practice at home has another advantage. It serves to set an example for the children so that, when they are ready for the responsibility of responsibility-evasion in their own business lives, they will not start as far back in the pack as you did. As a result, they may never need to read a book like this in order to learn what they must know if they are to be successful enough in business to keep you in comfort in your declining years.

Now that you know the rules, you know all you need to know to become a business leader. You know the Golden Secret that has taken men and women far less qualified than you to the pinnacle.

All hail Dodge #9.

The art of responsibility is evasion

Author's Postscript

The author feels it is only fair to disclose that, in submitting his manuscript to a large number of eminent and successful men and women for comment, suggestions and opinion, he has discovered (to his surprise) that there are two widely divergent interpretations of the text.

One group accepts the book as a serious behavioral guide to success in American business and political life. There is no question that those who fall into this category are the caliber of person who will most benefit from the protection that a literal interpretation of these rules will provide.

But a second group of critics have interpreted this book as a sly satire of certain business practices in our corporate society. They see this book not as a text but as a barbed criticism-in-reverse of what many regard as the greatest failure of modern corporate organizations—the headlong flight from responsibility of any kind. It is hoped that this group, too, will derive some benefit from a study of the rules and suggestions offered in this book.

Where does the author stand with respect to this controversy? Does he regard his work as a legitimate textbook or as a satire of some kind? Frankly, the author has not made a decision about this issue. Nor does he intend to.

He will however, appoint a committee to look into this matter and report back in 90 days.

Appendix A

The Dodges — Nine Ways to Avoid Paying the Piper

A dodge is an out, an excuse, a way to avoid paying the piper.

All of us are faced in life with situations we'd like to get out of, guilt we wish belonged to others, responsibilities we'd like to avoid. To allow us to do that, we have all perfected certain dodges we use in uncomfortable situations.

After a career in business, the author has discovered that there are nine general categories of dodges. We have listed them here, together with quotes that are common to each.

However, it is the last of these dodges, Dodge #9, that is the most important for anyone seeking success in the world of business and commerce. For anyone who can master Dodge #9, the other eight dodges are unnecessary. That's why this book has been written.

The Nine Dodges

1. *Ignorance:* Pretending that you know nothing about the matter at hand.

   "Did you mean me?"

   "Oh, is this yours?"

   "Was I supposed to do that?"

2. *Ingenuousness:* Being naïve, innocent.

"I'm not the one in charge here."

"I thought you knew."

"Was it my turn?"

3. *Denial:* Sometimes aggressive refusal to accept blame.

"I didn't do it."

"Who, me?"

"You must be thinking of Joe."

4. *Self Preservation:* Finger-pointing to avoid being tagged.

"It was Mary, not me."

"I was never told."

"How can you expect me to…."

5. *Shifting Blame:* Finding someone else to do it.

"The ball is in your court."

"You mean Annie, not me."

"I had nothing to do with that!"

6. *Time Consumption:* Putting off blame by postponing discussion.

"Let's do lunch sometime and talk about it."

"Call me when you have time."

"Why don't we wait till things settle down?"

7. *Finding Allies:* There is cover in company.

"If it's OK with you, I'll go along."

"Why don't we do it together?"

"I know John (Joe, Jean, etc.) will agree."

8. *Sheer Blindness:* Pretended inability to understand the situation.

"But I didn't know that."

"Nobody told me."

"What are you talking about?"

9. *Avoiding Decisions:* Foisting decisions on someone else.

"You decide. I'm too busy."

"I really need your wise counsel on this."

"I'll have one of the kids work on it."

Appendix B

Take This Quiz to See What You've Learned

Are you ready for the Big Time? Have you learned what you need to know to use Dodge #9—to never make a mistake because you never make a decision? Answer these questions and we'll just see about that.

1. The situation: You are driving the car pool gang to work and want to make a left at the next intersection. Do you...

a. Stick your left hand out of the window to signal a left turn?

b. Ask the front seat passenger to stick his hand out of his window and turn right instead of left? Turning right is obviously the wrong decision, but it isn't your fault.

c. Turn on your hazard flashers and go halfway up the block, then U-turn back and make a right when you reach the chosen intersection?

2. The situation: You are put in charge of leasing a fleet of automobiles for company executives to use in the coming year. Do you...

a. Take several months, carefully research the market and buy a sensible flock of mid-size Fords.

b. Lease a Ferrari convertible for the CEO and a bunch of used Escorts for everyone else?

c. Have young Smythe do the job and complain loudly to everyone no matter what he leases?

3. The situation: Cooper, Price-Waterhouse and Lybrand have done a comprehensive audit of your company's financial health and recommended a detailed list of steps to be taken to remedy a perilous financial situation. You are assigned the task of implementing CPL's advice. Do you...

a. Accept all of their recommendations and be done with it? After all, CPL is responsible, not you.

b. Review the list of suggested steps and delete any that might cause discomfort to any of your superiors, then implement the rest?

c. Assign the task to a pretty young accountant in your department and hope that her good looks and bright innocent smile will save her when, whatever she decides to do, turns out to be wrong.

4. How do you achieve success in corporate America?

a. Be a decisive leader of men.

b. Make only correct decisions.

c. Make no decisions at all.

5. What is the second most feared set of words in the business language?

a. Well, that's an interesting point of view, but....

b. You're fired!

c. You are responsible for this!

6. Which of these three people got to the top by making correct decisions?

  a. Bob Dole.

  b. Garry Hart.

  c. William Jefferson Clinton.

7. When assigning seats on the dais for your company's annual awards banquet, whom do you place to the immediate right of the CEO?

  a. The executive vice president.

  b. Yourself.

  c. Whoever grabs that chair first.

8. When in making a presentation in a budget meeting, the CFO seems to have forgotten what six times seven equals (42!), what do you do?

  a. Lean over and quietly correct him.

  b. Lean over and quietly alert the CEO to the error.

  c. Accept that six times seven now equals 47 and move on.

9. The young brand manager you are working to please objects to the sideburns worn by one of your subalterns. Do you…

  a. Tell him it is none of his business and move on to other matters.

  b. Agree with him and tell him you will speak to the offending young person.

  c. Pretend you didn't hear his complaint and ignore it completely.

Well, do you think you're ready for the big time in the world of business? Or should you read this whole damned book again?

THE END